THE BEGINNERS

AIR FRYER

COOKBOOK

From Zero to Air Fryer Hero: Easy Recipes for Beginners

JONELLE R JACKSON

TABLE OF CONTENTS

Welcome to Air Frying

Benefits of Air Frying:

1. Less Oil: Air frying uses up to 50% less oil than traditional deep-frying methods.
2. Healthier: By using less oil, air frying reduces the calorie and fat content of your food.
3. Easy to Use: Air fryers are simple to operate and require minimal cleanup.
4. Versatile: Air fryers are not just limited to frying foods. You can also use them to grill, roast, and bake.

Tips for Air Frying:

1. Pat Dry Excess Moisture: Remove excess moisture from food before air frying to ensure crispy results.
2. Use the Right Temperature: Adjust the temperature according to the type of food you're cooking.
3. Don't Overcrowd: Cook food in batches to ensure even cooking and prevent steaming.
4. Shake the Basket: Shake the basket halfway through cooking to ensure even cooking and crispy results.

Popular Air Fryer Recipes:

1. Chicken Wings: Marinate chicken wings in your favorite sauce and air fry until crispy.
2. French Fries: Slice potatoes into your favorite fry shape and air fry until crispy.
3. Shrimp: Marinate shrimp in your favorite seasonings and air fry until pink and crispy.
4. Veggie Fries: Slice your favorite vegetables into fry shapes and air fry until crispy.

Getting Started with Air Frying:

1. Choose an Air Fryer: Select an air fryer that suits your needs and budget.
2. Read the Manual: Familiarize yourself with the air fryer's settings and features.
3. Experiment with Recipes: Try out different recipes and seasonings to find your favorite air-fried dishes.

Benefits of Using an Air Fryer

Health Benefits
1. Less Oil: Air fryers use little to no oil, making them a healthier alternative to deep-frying.
2. Lower Calorie Count: With less oil, air-fried foods have fewer calories, making them ideal for weight management.
3. Reduced Fat Content: Air fryers help reduce the fat content of food, making them a great option for those with high cholesterol or heart health concerns.

Convenience Benefits
1. Easy to Use: Air fryers are simple to operate, with most models featuring preset buttons and intuitive controls.
2. Fast Cooking Times: Air fryers cook food quickly, with most dishes ready in under 20 minutes.
3. Cleaning is Easy: Air fryers are relatively easy to clean, with most parts dishwasher safe.

Versatility Benefits
1. Multi-Functional: Air fryers are not just limited to frying food. They can also grill, roast, and bake.
2. Wide Range of Recipes: Air fryers can be used to cook a wide variety of dishes, from snacks to main courses.
3. Experiment with New Recipes: Air fryers allow you to experiment with new recipes and cooking techniques.

Cost Benefits
1. Energy Efficient: Air fryers use less energy than traditional deep fryers, making them a cost-effective option.
2. Long-Lasting: Air fryers are built to last, with many models featuring durable construction and long-lasting parts.
3. Less Oil Consumption: With air fryers, you'll use less oil, which can save you money in the long run.

Environmental Benefits
1. Reduced Waste: Air fryers produce less waste than traditional deep fryers, as they use less oil and packaging.
2. Energy Savings: By using less energy, air fryers help reduce your carbon footprint and contribute to a more sustainable future.
3. Healthier Cooking Options: Air fryers promote healthier cooking options, which can lead to a reduction in food-related waste and environmental harm.

Air Fryer Safety Tips

Before First Use
1. Read the manual: Familiarize yourself with the air fryer's settings, features, and safety precautions.
2. Inspect the air fryer: Check for any damage or defects before using the air fryer.

General Safety Precautions
1. Place on a stable surface: Ensure the air fryer is on a flat, stable surface, away from children and pets.
2. Keep away from water: Avoid placing the air fryer near water sources, such as sinks or dishwashers.
3. Use oven mitts: Handle the air fryer basket and pan with oven mitts to prevent burns.
4. Avoid overheating: Don't leave the air fryer unattended, as overheating can cause a fire.
5. Clean regularly: Regularly clean the air fryer to prevent food buildup and bacterial growth.

Cooking Safety
1. Pat dry excess moisture: Remove excess moisture from food before cooking to prevent splatters and burns.
2. Use the right temperature: Adjust the temperature according to the type of food you're cooking.
3. Don't overcrowd: Cook food in batches to ensure even cooking and prevent steaming.
4. Shake the basket: Shake the basket halfway through cooking to ensure even cooking and crispy results.

Electrical Safety
1. Use the correct power source: Plug the air fryer into a grounded outlet to prevent electrical shock.
2. Avoid extension cords: Use the air fryer's built-in cord instead of extension cords to prevent overheating.
3. Unplug when not in use: Unplug the air fryer when not in use to prevent accidents and conserve energy.

Additional Safety Tips
1. Keep children away: Keep children away from the air fryer while it's in use.
2. Use air fryer accessories: Use air fryer accessories, such as a splatter guard, to prevent hot oil splatters.
3. Follow recipe guidelines: Follow recipe guidelines and cooking times to prevent overcooking or undercooking.

Choosing the Right Air Fryer

Considerations:

1. Size and Capacity: How much food do you plan to cook at once? Choose an air fryer that suits your needs, from compact 2-quart models to larger 6-quart ones.
2. Power and Performance: Look for an air fryer with a powerful motor (around 1700 watts) and multiple heat settings (up to 400°F) for optimal performance.
3. Features and Presets: Some air fryers come with preset buttons for specific dishes, such as fries or chicken. Consider an air fryer with features like dehydrate, grill, or slow cook.
4. Ease of Use and Cleaning: Opt for an air fryer with a user-friendly interface, dishwasher-safe parts, and a non-stick basket for easy cleaning.
5. Brand and Warranty: Research reputable brands and look for air fryers with a comprehensive warranty (at least 1 year) and good customer support.
6. Price: Air fryers vary in price, from under $100 to over $300. Set a budget and balance it with the features and performance you need.

Types of Air Fryers:

1. Basket-Style Air Fryers: These are the most common type, featuring a basket and a compact design.
2. Tray-Style Air Fryers: These have a larger cooking surface and are ideal for cooking multiple items at once.
3. Multifunctional Air Fryers: These air fryers come with additional features like slow cooking, dehydrating, or pressure cooking.

Top Brands:

1. Philips: Known for their high-quality and innovative air fryers.
2. GoWISE USA: Offers a range of affordable and feature-rich air fryers.
3. Black+Decker: Provides compact and easy-to-use air fryers.
4. Ninja: Famous for their high-performance and multifunctional air fryers.

Final Tips:

1. Read Reviews: Check out reviews from other customers to get a sense of an air fryer's performance and any potential issues.
2. Compare Features: Make a list of the features you need and compare them across different air fryer models.
3. Check the Warranty: Ensure the air fryer you choose has a comprehensive warranty that covers repairs and replacements.

How to Use This Cookbook

1. Recipe Title: The name of the dish, along with a brief description.
2. Servings: The number of people the recipe serves.
3. Cooking Time: The estimated time it takes to cook the recipe.
4. Ingredients: A list of ingredients needed for the recipe.
5. Instructions: Step-by-step instructions on how to prepare and cook the recipe.
6. Tips and Variations: Additional tips, variations, and suggestions to help you customize the recipe.

Converting Recipes:

If you need to convert a recipe to suit your dietary needs or preferences, here are some general guidelines:

1. Vegetarian/Vegan: Replace meat with plant-based alternatives, such as tofu, tempeh, or seitan.
2. Gluten-Free: Replace gluten-containing ingredients with gluten-free alternatives.
3. Low-Sodium: Reduce or omit added salt, and use low-sodium ingredients.

Air Fryer Tips and Tricks:

To get the most out of your air fryer, keep the following tips in mind:

1. Pat dry excess moisture: Remove excess moisture from ingredients before cooking to ensure crispy results.
2. Don't overcrowd: Cook ingredients in batches to prevent steaming and ensure even cooking.
3. Shake the basket: Shake the basket halfway through cooking to ensure even cooking and crispy results.

Measurement Conversions:

For your convenience, here are some common measurement conversions:

1. Teaspoons to Tablespoons: 1 teaspoon = 3 tablespoons
2. Tablespoons to Cups: 1 tablespoon = 1/16 cup
3. Celsius to Fahrenheit: 1°C = 33.8°F

Ingredient Substitutions:

If you don't have a specific ingredient, here are some common substitutions:

1. Baking powder: 1 teaspoon baking powder = 1 1/2 teaspoons baking soda + 1/2 teaspoon cream of tartar
2. Buttermilk: 1 cup buttermilk = 1 cup milk + 1 tablespoon white vinegar or lemon juice

Key Ingredients and Substitutes

Proteins
1. Chicken: Breast, thighs, wings, or tenders work well in the air fryer.
2. Beef: Thinly sliced beef (e.g., ribeye, sirloin) or beef strips are ideal.
3. Pork: Pork chops, pork belly, or carnitas can be cooked to perfection.
4. Fish: Delicate fish like salmon, tilapia, or cod work well in the air fryer.
5. Tofu: Extra-firm tofu, drained and cut into cubes or slices, is a great option.

Vegetables
1. Potatoes: Thinly sliced potatoes or potato wedges are perfect for air frying.
2. Sweet Potatoes: Similar to regular potatoes, sweet potatoes can be sliced or wedged.
3. Broccoli: Florets or stalks can be air-fried to a tender, crispy texture.
4. Cauliflower: Like broccoli, cauliflower florets or stalks work well in the air fryer.
5. Onions: Sliced or chopped onions can be air-fried to a caramelized, crispy texture.

Grains and Starches
1. Bread: Sliced bread, breadsticks, or croutons can be air-fried to a crispy texture.
2. Pasta: Some air fryer models come with a pasta basket, allowing for perfectly cooked pasta.
3. Rice: Cooked rice can be air-fried to a crispy texture, making it a great base for dishes like fried rice.

Substitutes and Alternatives
1. Gluten-free alternatives: For gluten-free diets, substitute bread with gluten-free options or use cauliflower crusts.
2. Vegan substitutes: Replace eggs with flaxseed or chia seeds, and use plant-based milk alternatives.
3. Low-sodium options: Use herbs and spices to add flavor instead of salt, and opt for low-sodium sauces.
4. Sugar-free alternatives: Replace sugar with natural sweeteners like honey, maple syrup, or stevia.

Essential Pantry Staples
1. Oils: Avocado oil, olive oil, or coconut oil for air frying and adding flavor.
2. Spices: Salt, pepper, garlic powder, paprika, and any other spices you prefer.
3. Herbs: Fresh or dried herbs like thyme, rosemary, or basil add flavor to dishes.
4. Sauces and marinades: Store-bought or homemade sauces and marinades can elevate your air fryer dishes.

Understanding Cooking Times and Temperatures

Factors Affecting Cooking Times and Temperatures:

1. Type and Quality of Ingredients: Freshness, size, and density of ingredients can impact cooking times and temperatures.
2. Air Fryer Model and Size: Different air fryer models and sizes can have varying cooking times and temperatures.
3. Cooking Method and Technique: Cooking methods, such as marinating or breading, can affect cooking times and temperatures.
4. Desired Level of Doneness: Cooking times and temperatures can vary depending on the desired level of doneness, such as rare, medium, or well-done.

General Cooking Time and Temperature Guidelines:

1. Proteins:
    - Chicken: 375°F (190°C), 10-15 minutes
    - Beef: 400°F (200°C), 10-15 minutes
    - Fish: 400°F (200°C), 8-12 minutes
2. Vegetables:
    - Leafy Greens: 300°F (150°C), 5-7 minutes
    - Root Vegetables: 400°F (200°C), 15-20 minutes
    - Cruciferous Vegetables: 375°F (190°C), 10-15 minutes
3. Snacks and Appetizers:
    - French Fries: 400°F (200°C), 10-12 minutes
    - Chicken Wings: 400°F (200°C), 20-25 minutes

Tips for Adjusting Cooking Times and Temperatures:

1. Use a Food Thermometer: Ensure your ingredients are cooked to a safe internal temperature.
2. Don't Overcrowd: Cook ingredients in batches to prevent steaming and ensure even cooking.
3. Shake the Basket: Shake the basket halfway through cooking to ensure even cooking and crispy results.
4. Keep an Eye on It: Monitor your ingredients during cooking and adjust cooking times and temperatures as needed.

Chapter 1

Getting Started

Unpacking and Setting Up Your Air Fryer

Serving Size: N/A
Cooking Time: N/A
Prep Time: 10-15 minutes
Nutrition Info: N/A
Ingredients: N/A
Directions:

1. Unpacking: Carefully remove the air fryer from its packaging and discard the box and packing materials.
2. Inspecting the Air Fryer: Check the air fryer for any damage or defects. Make sure all parts, including the basket, pan, and accessories, are included.
3. Washing the Parts: Wash the basket, pan, and any other accessories with warm soapy water. Rinse thoroughly and dry with a towel.
4. Assembling the Air Fryer: Follow the manufacturer's instructions to assemble the air fryer. Typically, this involves attaching the basket to the pan and placing the pan into the air fryer unit.
5. Plugging in the Air Fryer: Plug in the air fryer and place it on a flat, stable surface.
6. Setting the Temperature and Timer: Familiarize yourself with the air fryer's controls and set the temperature and timer according to the manufacturer's instructions.
7. Testing the Air Fryer: Before cooking, test the air fryer by running it empty for a few minutes to ensure it's working correctly.

Tips and Precautions:

- Always follow the manufacturer's instructions for unpacking, assembling, and using your air fryer.
- Make sure the air fryer is placed on a stable surface, away from children and pets.
- Never leave the air fryer unattended while it's in operation.
- Always wash your hands before and after handling food and the air fryer.

Essential Tools and Accessories

Essential Tools:
1. Tongs or Slotted Spoon: For easy food handling and turning.
2. Silicone Mat: For lining the air fryer basket and preventing food from sticking.
3. Oven Mitts: For protecting your hands from burns when handling the air fryer basket.
4. Kitchen Shears: For cutting ingredients and portioning food.

Essential Accessories:
1. Air Fryer Basket Divider: For separating ingredients and cooking multiple foods at once.
2. Air Fryer Grill Pan: For grilling and searing ingredients.
3. Air Fryer Pizza Pan: For cooking pizzas and other flatbreads.
4. Air Fryer Recipe Book: For inspiration and guidance on new air fryer recipes.

Serving Size: N/A
Cooking Time: N/A
Prep Time: N/A
Nutrition Info: N/A
Ingredients: N/A
Directions:
1. Invest in the essential tools and accessories listed above.
2. Familiarize yourself with each tool and accessory.
3. Experiment with new recipes and cooking techniques using your air fryer and accessories.

- Preheating and Cooking Basics

Serving Size: N/A
Cooking Time: Varies
Prep Time: 5 minutes
Nutrition Info: N/A
Ingredients: N/A
Directions:
Preheating Basics
1. Read the manual: Familiarize yourself with your air fryer's preheating instructions.
2. Set the temperature: Choose the recommended temperature for your recipe.
3. Preheat the air fryer: Allow the air fryer to preheat for 2-5 minutes, depending on the model and temperature.

4. Check the preheat indicator: Wait for the preheat indicator (e.g., light, beep) to signal that the air fryer is ready.

Cooking Basics
1. Pat dry excess moisture: Remove excess moisture from ingredients to ensure crispy results.
2. Load the basket: Place ingredients in a single layer, leaving space for air circulation.
3. Cooking time and temperature: Adjust cooking time and temperature according to your recipe and the air fryer's guidelines.
4. Shake the basket: Shake the basket halfway through cooking to ensure even cooking and crispy results.
5. Check for doneness: Verify that your food is cooked to your desired level of doneness.

Tips and Variations
- Experiment with marinades and seasonings: Add flavor to your dishes with marinades, rubs, and seasonings.
- Don't overcrowd: Cook ingredients in batches to prevent steaming and ensure even cooking.
- Clean the air fryer regularly: Maintain your air fryer's performance by cleaning it after each use.

Air Fryer Functions Explained

Functions and Settings
1. Temperature Control: Adjust the temperature (usually between 175°F to 400°F) to suit the type of food being cooked.
2. Timer: Set the cooking time (usually up to 60 minutes) to ensure your food is cooked to perfection.
3. Presets: Use pre-programmed settings for specific foods, such as fries, chicken, or steak.
4. Manual Mode: Override presets and adjust temperature and timer manually.
5. Dehydrate Function: Use low temperatures (usually around 135°F) to dehydrate fruits, vegetables, or meats.
6. Grill Function: Achieve grill marks and crispy textures using high temperatures (usually around 400°F).
7. Keep Warm Function: Maintain a consistent temperature (usually around 175°F) to keep cooked food warm.

Serving Size: N/A
Cooking Time: N/A
Prep Time: N/A
Nutrition Info: N/A
Ingredients: N/A
Directions:
1. Read the manual: Familiarize yourself with your air fryer's specific functions and settings.

2. Experiment with presets: Try out pre-programmed settings for different foods.

3. Adjust manually: Override presets to customize cooking time and temperature.

4. Explore additional functions: Use dehydrate, grill, and keep warm functions to expand your cooking repertoire.

First-Time Cooking Tips

Serving Size: N/A

Cooking Time: N/A

Prep Time: 10 minutes

Nutrition Info: N/A

Ingredients: N/A

Directions:

Before You Start

1. Read the manual: Familiarize yourself with your air fryer's specific features and settings.

2. Wash and dry the basket: Clean the basket and pan before first use.

Cooking Essentials

1. Pat dry excess moisture: Remove excess moisture from ingredients to ensure crispy results.

2. Don't overcrowd: Cook ingredients in batches to prevent steaming and ensure even cooking.

3. Shake the basket: Shake the basket halfway through cooking to ensure even cooking and crispy results.

Safety First

1. Use oven mitts: Protect your hands from burns when handling the air fryer basket.

2. Keep children away: Ensure children are at a safe distance from the air fryer while it's in operation.

Troubleshooting

1. Food not crispy?: Check temperature and cooking time. Adjust as needed.

2. Food overcooked?: Reduce cooking time and temperature for next use.

Cleaning and Maintenance

Serving Size: N/A
Cooking Time: N/A
Prep Time: 10-15 minutes
Nutrition Info: N/A
Ingredients:
- Soft sponge or cloth
- Mild dish soap
- Warm water
- Dry towel
- Optional: Baking soda, vinegar, or a mixture of equal parts water and white vinegar

Directions:
Daily Cleaning:
1. Unplug the air fryer and let it cool down completely.
2. Remove the basket and pan, and wash them with mild dish soap and warm water.
3. Dry the basket and pan thoroughly with a dry towel.
4. Wipe down the exterior of the air fryer with a damp cloth.

Deep Cleaning:
1. Mix 1 tablespoon of baking soda with 1 tablespoon of water to create a paste.
2. Apply the paste to the basket and pan, and let it sit for 30 minutes.
3. Rinse the basket and pan with warm water, and dry them thoroughly.
4. For tougher stains, mix equal parts water and white vinegar in the basket. Let it sit for 30 minutes before rinsing and drying.

Maintenance Tips:
1. Regularly check and clean the air fryer's filter to ensure optimal performance.
2. Avoid using abrasive cleaners or scouring pads, as they can damage the air fryer's non-stick coating.
3. Dry the air fryer thoroughly after cleaning to prevent water spots.

Storage and Care for Longevity

Serving Size: N/A
Cooking Time: N/A
Prep Time: 5 minutes
Nutrition Info: N/A
Ingredients: N/A
Directions:

Storage Tips:
1. Clean before storing: Ensure the air fryer is clean and dry before storing.
2. Store in a dry place: Keep the air fryer away from moisture and humidity.
3. Avoid direct sunlight: Store the air fryer in a shaded area to prevent damage from direct sunlight.
4. Use the original packaging: If possible, store the air fryer in its original packaging to protect it from dust and damage.

Caring for Your Air Fryer:
1. Regular cleaning: Clean the air fryer regularly to prevent food buildup and bacterial growth.
2. Avoid abrasive cleaners: Use gentle cleaners and soft cloths to prevent damage to the air fryer's non-stick coating.
3. Dry thoroughly: Dry the air fryer thoroughly after cleaning to prevent water spots.
4. Check for wear and tear: Regularly inspect the air fryer for signs of wear and tear, and replace worn-out parts as needed.

Additional Tips:
1. Refer to the user manual: Consult the user manual for specific storage and care instructions for your air fryer model.
2. Avoid stacking: Avoid stacking objects on top of the air fryer to prevent damage.
3. Keep it away from children: Store the air fryer in a secure location, out of reach of children.

Chapter 2

Breakfast Delights

Perfectly Cooked Eggs

Serving Size: 1-2 eggs
Cooking Time: 5-7 minutes
Prep Time: 2 minutes
Nutrition Info (per egg):
``` Calories: 70
Protein: 6g
Fat: 5g
Cholesterol: 186mg
```

Ingredients:
``` 1-2 eggs
Salt and pepper to taste
Cooking spray or oil (optional)
```

Directions:
1. Preheat the air fryer to 250°F (120°C).
2. Crack the egg(s) into a small bowl or ramekin.
3. Add a pinch of salt and pepper to taste.
4. If desired, spray the air fryer basket with cooking spray or brush with oil.
5. Place the egg(s) in the air fryer basket.
6. Cook for 5-7 minutes, or until the whites are set and the yolks are cooked to your desired doneness.
7. Remove the egg(s) from the air fryer and serve hot.

Tips and Variations:

- For a runnier yolk, cook for 5 minutes. For a firmer yolk, cook for 7 minutes.
- Add a sprinkle of shredded cheese or chopped herbs for extra flavor.
- Cook multiple eggs at once by placing them in a single layer in the air fryer basket.
- Experiment with different seasonings, such as paprika or chili powder, for added flavor.

Air Fryer Pancakes

Serving Size: 4-6 pancakes
Cooking Time: 4-6 minutes
Prep Time: 10 minutes
Nutrition Info (per pancake):
```

Calories: 120
Protein: 2g
Fat: 2g
Carbohydrates: 25g
```

Ingredients:
```

1 cup all-purpose flour
2 tablespoons sugar
2 teaspoons baking powder
1/4 teaspoon salt
1 cup milk
1 large egg
2 tablespoons melted butter
Optional: blueberries, chocolate chips, or other mix-ins
```

Directions:
1. In a large bowl, whisk together flour, sugar, baking powder, and salt.
2. In a separate bowl, whisk together milk, egg, and melted butter.
3. Add the wet ingredients to the dry ingredients and stir until just combined. Do not overmix.
4. If desired, add mix-ins such as blueberries or chocolate chips.
5. Pour 1/4 cup of batter onto the air fryer basket, leaving about 1 inch of space between each pancake.
6. Cook in the air fryer at 375°F (190°C) for 4-6 minutes, or until bubbles appear on the surface and the edges are golden brown.
7. Flip the pancakes and cook for an additional 1-2 minutes, or until the other side is also golden brown.
8. Serve hot with your favorite toppings, such as syrup, butter, or fresh fruit.

Tips and Variations:

- Use a non-stick air fryer basket or spray with cooking spray to prevent sticking.
- Experiment with different mix-ins, such as nuts, cinnamon, or vanilla extract.
- For a crisper exterior, cook the pancakes at a higher temperature (400°F/200°C) for a shorter amount of time (3-4 minutes).
- Make a batch of pancake batter ahead of time and store it in the fridge for up to 24 hours.

Crispy Bacon

Serving Size: 4-6 slices
Cooking Time: 5-7 minutes
Prep Time: 2 minutes
Nutrition Info (per 2 slices):
```

Calories: 120
Protein: 10g
Fat: 9g
Sodium: 450mg
```

Ingredients:
```

4-6 slices of bacon (thicker cuts work best)
Optional: brown sugar, smoked paprika, or other seasonings
```

Directions:
1. Preheat the air fryer to 400°F (200°C).
2. Line the air fryer basket with parchment paper or a silicone mat.
3. Lay the bacon slices in a single layer, leaving some space between each slice.
4. Cook the bacon for 5-7 minutes, or until crispy and golden brown.
5. Flip the bacon halfway through cooking for even crispiness.
6. Remove the bacon from the air fryer and place it on a paper towel-lined plate to drain excess grease.
7. Optional: sprinkle with brown sugar, smoked paprika, or other seasonings for added flavor.

Tips and Variations:

- Use thicker cuts of bacon for the crispiest results.
- Experiment with different seasonings, such as garlic powder, chili powder, or maple syrup.
- Cook the bacon in batches if necessary, to ensure even cooking.
- Store leftover crispy bacon in an airtight container for up to 3 days.

Breakfast Burritos

Serving Size: 2-4 burritos
Cooking Time: 5-7 minutes
Prep Time: 10 minutes

Nutrition Info (per burrito):
```

Calories: 350
Protein: 20g
Fat: 15g
Carbohydrates: 30g
```

Ingredients:
```

4 large eggs
4 slices of bacon
1 cup shredded cheese (Cheddar or Monterey Jack work well)
4 large tortillas
Salt and pepper to taste
Optional: diced bell peppers, onions, salsa, or sour cream
```

Directions:
1. Cook the bacon in the air fryer at 400°F (200°C) for 5-7 minutes, or until crispy.
2. In a bowl, whisk together the eggs and a pinch of salt. Pour the egg mixture into a greased air fryer basket.
3. Cook the scrambled eggs in the air fryer at 300°F (150°C) for 2-3 minutes, or until set.
4. Warm the tortillas by wrapping them in a damp paper towel and microwaving for 20-30 seconds.
5. Assemble the burritos by filling each tortilla with scrambled eggs, crispy bacon, and shredded cheese.
6. Add any desired optional fillings, such as diced bell peppers or salsa.
7. Fold the tortillas to enclose the fillings and serve hot.

Tips and Variations:

- Use leftover cooked sausage, ham, or black beans for added protein.
- Experiment with different types of cheese, such as Pepper Jack or Queso Fresco.
- Add diced veggies, such as mushrooms or zucchini, to the scrambled eggs for added nutrition.
- Store leftover burritos in an airtight container for up to 2 days and reheat in the air fryer or microwave.

French Toast Sticks

Serving Size: 4-6 sticks
Cooking Time: 4-6 minutes
Prep Time: 5 minutes

Nutrition Info (per serving):
```

Calories: 150
Protein: 4g
Fat: 3g
Carbohydrates: 25g
```

Ingredients:
```

4-6 slices of bread (preferably challah or brioche)
2 large eggs
1 cup milk
1/4 cup granulated sugar
1/4 teaspoon ground cinnamon
2 tablespoons unsalted butter, melted
Optional: maple syrup, fresh fruit, or whipped cream
```

Directions:
1. In a shallow dish, whisk together eggs, milk, sugar, and cinnamon.
2. Dip each bread slice into the egg mixture, coating both sides evenly.
3. Place the coated bread slices in a single layer in the air fryer basket.
4. Cook the French toast sticks in the air fryer at 375°F (190°C) for 4-6 minutes, or until golden brown.
5. Flip the sticks halfway through cooking for even browning.
6. Remove the French toast sticks from the air fryer and serve hot with melted butter and desired toppings.

Tips and Variations:

- Use leftover bread to make French toast sticks.
- Experiment with different types of bread, such as croissants or baguettes.
- Add a sprinkle of cinnamon or nutmeg on top of the French toast sticks before cooking.
- Serve with a side of fresh fruit or whipped cream for a delicious breakfast treat.

Air Fryer Granola

Serving Size: 1/4 cup
Cooking Time: 5-7 minutes
Prep Time: 5 minutes

Nutrition Info (per serving):
```

Calories: 120
Protein: 2g
Fat: 2g
Carbohydrates: 25g
Fiber: 2g
```

Ingredients:
```

2 cups rolled oats
1 cup mixed nuts (almonds, cashews, walnuts)
1/2 cup honey
2 tablespoons maple syrup
1/4 cup vegetable oil
1 teaspoon vanilla extract
Pinch of salt
Optional: dried fruits (cranberries, raisins, cherries)
```

Directions:
1. In a large bowl, mix together oats, nuts, and salt.
2. In a separate bowl, whisk together honey, maple syrup, and vegetable oil.
3. Pour the wet ingredients over the dry ingredients and stir until everything is well combined.
4. Add vanilla extract and mix well.
5. Pour the granola mixture into the air fryer basket in a single layer.
6. Cook in the air fryer at 250°F (120°C) for 5-7 minutes, stirring every 2 minutes, until lightly toasted.
7. Remove from the air fryer and let cool completely.
8. Add dried fruits (if using) and mix well.
9. Store in an airtight container for up to 2 weeks.

Tips and Variations:

- Customize with your favorite nuts, seeds, or dried fruits.
- Use coconut oil or avocado oil for a different flavor.
- Add a sprinkle of cinnamon or nutmeg for extra spice.
- Make a batch of granola bars by pressing the mixture into a lined baking dish and refrigerating until set.

Savory Breakfast Muffins

Serving Size: 6-8 muffins
Cooking Time: 12-15 minutes
Prep Time: 10 minutes

Nutrition Info (per muffin):
```

Calories: 220
Protein: 12g
Fat: 10g
Carbohydrates: 20g
Fiber: 2g
```

Ingredients:
```

1 1/2 cups all-purpose flour
1 cup grated cheddar cheese
1/2 cup diced ham or bacon
1/2 cup diced bell peppers
1/2 cup diced onions
2 large eggs
1/2 cup milk
1/4 cup chopped fresh parsley
Salt and pepper to taste
```

Directions:
1. Preheat the air fryer to 375°F (190°C).
2. In a large bowl, whisk together flour, cheese, ham or bacon, bell peppers, and onions.
3. In a separate bowl, whisk together eggs, milk, and parsley.
4. Add the wet ingredients to the dry ingredients and stir until just combined.
5. Divide the batter evenly among 6-8 muffin cups.
6. Cook the muffins in the air fryer for 12-15 minutes, or until golden brown and cooked through.
7. Remove from the air fryer and let cool for a few minutes.
8. Serve warm and enjoy!

Tips and Variations:

- Customize with your favorite ingredients, such as diced sausage or mushrooms.
- Use different types of cheese, such as Swiss or feta.
- Add a sprinkle of chopped fresh herbs, such as chives or thyme.
- Make a batch of mini muffins for a quick and easy breakfast snack.

Chapter 3

Appetizers and Snacks

Classic French Fries

Servings: 4-6 people

Cooking Time: 20-25 minutes

Prep Time: 30 minutes

Nutrition Information (per serving):

- Calories: 170
- Fat: 9g
- Saturated Fat: 1.5g
- Sodium: 200mg
- Carbohydrates: 20g
- Fiber: 2g
- Sugar: 0g
- Protein: 2g

Ingredients:

- 2-3 large potatoes
- 1/2 cup vegetable oil
- 1/2 teaspoon salt
- 1/4 teaspoon black pepper
- 1/4 teaspoon garlic powder (optional)
- 1/4 teaspoon paprika (optional)

Directions:

1. Select and peel the potatoes: Choose potatoes that are high in starch, like Russet or Idaho. Peel the potatoes using a vegetable peeler or a sharp knife.

2. Cut the potatoes: Cut the peeled potatoes into long, thin strips. You can either cut them by hand or use a French fry cutter. Try to make the cuts as uniform as possible so that the fries cook evenly.

1. Soak the potatoes: Fill a large bowl with cold water and add a handful of ice cubes. Submerge the cut potatoes in the ice water and let them soak for at least 30 minutes. This step helps remove excess starch from the potatoes, resulting in crisper fries.

2. Heat the oil: Fill a large pot or deep fryer with vegetable oil. Heat the oil to around 350°F (175°C) for conventional potatoes or 325°F (165°C) for sweet potatoes.

1. Double-fry the potatoes: Double-frying is a technique that involves frying the potatoes twice to achieve the perfect crispiness. Here's how to do it:
   - First fry: Remove the potatoes from the ice water and pat them dry with paper towels to remove excess moisture. Carefully add the potatoes to the hot oil in batches, being careful not to overcrowd the pot. Fry the potatoes for around 3-5 minutes or until they are slightly tender and pale. Remove the potatoes from the oil with a slotted spoon and let them cool on a paper towel-lined plate for at least 30 minutes.
   - Second fry: Increase the oil temperature to around 375°F (190°C). Add the cooled potatoes back to the hot oil in batches and fry for an additional 2-3 minutes or until they are golden brown and crispy. Remove the fries from the oil with a slotted spoon and place them on a paper towel-lined plate to drain excess oil.

1. Season the fries: Sprinkle the French fries with salt, black pepper, garlic powder, and paprika (if using). Toss the fries gently to distribute the seasonings evenly.

1. Serve: Serve the classic French fries hot and enjoy! You can pair them with your favorite dipping sauce, such as ketchup, mayonnaise, or a homemade aioli.

Tips and Variations:

- For extra crispy fries, try soaking the potatoes in cold water for several hours or even overnight.
- To add extra flavor, try adding a few cloves of minced garlic or a sprinkle of grated cheese to the potatoes before frying.
- For a sweet potato version, use sweet potatoes instead of regular potatoes and adjust the cooking time accordingly.
- To bake the fries instead of frying, preheat your oven to 400°F (200°C) and bake the potatoes for around 20-25 minutes or until crispy.

Mozzarella Sticks

Serving Size: 4-6 sticks

Prep Time: 15 minutes

Cooking Time: 8-10 minutes

Total Time: 23-25 minutes

Nutrition Information (per serving):

- Calories: 220
- Fat: 12g
- Saturated Fat: 8g
- Cholesterol: 20mg
- Sodium: 350mg
- Carbohydrates: 20g
- Fiber: 0g
- Sugar: 0g
- Protein: 6g

Ingredients:

- 1 cup mozzarella cheese sticks (about 12-15 sticks)
- 1 cup all-purpose flour
- 1 teaspoon paprika
- 1/2 teaspoon garlic powder
- 1/2 teaspoon salt
- 1/4 teaspoon black pepper
- 2 eggs
- 1 cup breadcrumbs (Panko or regular)
- Vegetable oil for frying
- Marinara sauce for serving (optional)

Directions:

1. Prepare the breading station: In one shallow dish, mix together flour, paprika, garlic powder, salt, and pepper. In another dish, beat the eggs. In a third dish, place the breadcrumbs.
2. Prepare the cheese sticks: Cut the mozzarella cheese sticks in half, if desired, to make them easier to handle.

3. Bread the cheese sticks: Dip each cheese stick into the flour mixture, coating lightly, then into the eggs, making sure they're fully coated, and finally into the breadcrumbs, pressing the crumbs gently onto the cheese to help them stick. Place the breaded cheese sticks on a plate or tray.

4. Heat the oil: Heat about 1/2-inch (1 cm) of vegetable oil in a large skillet over medium-high heat until it reaches 350°F (175°C).

5. Fry the mozzarella sticks: Carefully place 3-4 breaded cheese sticks into the hot oil. Do not overcrowd the skillet. Fry for 2-3 minutes on each side, until golden brown and crispy. Repeat with the remaining cheese sticks.

6. Drain excess oil: Remove the fried mozzarella sticks from the oil with a slotted spoon and place them on a paper towel-lined plate to drain excess oil.

7. Serve: Serve the crispy mozzarella sticks hot with marinara sauce for dipping, if desired. Enjoy!

Tips:

- For an extra crispy coating, you can chill the breaded cheese sticks in the refrigerator for 30 minutes before frying.
- To bake instead of fry, preheat your oven to 400°F (200°C). Place the breaded cheese sticks on a baking sheet lined with parchment paper and bake for 10-12 minutes, until crispy and golden brown.

Chicken Wings

Serving Size: 4-6 people (about 20-25 wings)

Prep Time: 20 minutes

Cooking Time: 35-40 minutes

Total Time: 55-60 minutes

Nutrition Information (per serving):

- Calories: 320
- Fat: 22g
- Saturated Fat: 5g
- Cholesterol: 60mg
- Sodium: 450mg
- Carbohydrates: 0g
- Fiber: 0g
- Sugar: 0g
- Protein: 25g

Ingredients:

- 2 pounds chicken wings
- 1/2 cup all-purpose flour
- 1 teaspoon paprika
- 1 teaspoon garlic powder
- 1 teaspoon onion powder
- 1 teaspoon salt
- 1/2 teaspoon black pepper
- 1/4 teaspoon cayenne pepper (optional)
- 1/2 cup butter, melted
- Vegetable oil for frying
- Sauce of your choice (BBQ, Buffalo, Honey Mustard, etc.)

Directions:

1. Prep the wings: Rinse the chicken wings and pat them dry with paper towels.
2. Season the wings: In a large bowl, mix together flour, paprika, garlic powder, onion powder, salt, black pepper, and cayenne pepper (if using). Toss the chicken wings in the flour mixture to coat evenly.
3. Fry the wings: Heat about 2-3 inches (5-7.5 cm) of vegetable oil in a large pot or deep fryer to 375°F (190°C). Fry the chicken wings in batches until golden brown and crispy, about 8-10 minutes per batch. Repeat with the remaining wings.
4. Drain excess oil: Remove the fried chicken wings from the oil with a slotted spoon and place them on a paper towel-lined plate to drain excess oil.
5. Toss in sauce (optional): If desired, toss the fried chicken wings in your favorite sauce (BBQ, Buffalo, Honey Mustard, etc.).
6. Serve: Serve the crispy chicken wings hot with celery sticks and blue cheese dressing for a classic snack. Enjoy!

Tips:

- To bake instead of fry, preheat your oven to 400°F (200°C). Place the seasoned chicken wings on a baking sheet lined with parchment paper and bake for 25-30 minutes, until crispy and golden brown.
- For extra crispy wings, you can chill them in the refrigerator for 30 minutes before frying.
- Experiment with different seasonings and sauces to create unique flavor combinations.

Veggie Chips

Serving Size: 4-6 servings (about 1 cup chips)

Prep Time: 20 minutes

Cooking Time: 15-20 minutes

Total Time: 35-40 minutes

Nutrition Information (per serving):

- Calories: 120
- Fat: 3g
- Saturated Fat: 0g
- Sodium: 100mg
- Carbohydrates: 25g
- Fiber: 4g
- Sugar: 6g
- Protein: 2g

Ingredients:

- 2-3 large sweet potatoes or other root vegetables (such as beets, parsnips, or carrots)
- 1/2 cup olive oil
- Salt, to taste
- Optional: Additional seasonings, such as paprika, garlic powder, or chili powder

Directions:

1. Preheat the oven: Preheat the oven to 400°F (200°C).
2. Peel and slice the vegetables: Peel the sweet potatoes or other root vegetables and slice them into very thin rounds, using a mandoline or sharp knife.
3. Soak the slices: To remove excess starch and help the chips become crispy, soak the sliced vegetables in cold water for at least 30 minutes. After soaking, drain the slices and pat them dry with paper towels to remove excess moisture.
4. Toss with oil and seasonings: In a large bowl, toss the dried vegetable slices with olive oil, salt, and any additional desired seasonings until the slices are evenly coated.
5. Bake the chips: Line a baking sheet with parchment paper or a silicone mat. Arrange the vegetable slices in a single layer on the prepared baking sheet. Bake for 15-20 minutes, or until the chips are crispy and golden brown, flipping them halfway through the cooking time.

6. Serve: Remove the veggie chips from the oven and let them cool slightly on the baking sheet. Then, transfer them to a paper towel-lined plate to drain any excess moisture. Serve the delicious veggie chips warm, or let them cool completely and store them in an airtight container for up to 24 hours.

Tips:

- For an extra crispy texture, try baking the veggie chips at a higher temperature (425°F/220°C) for a shorter amount of time (10-12 minutes). Keep an eye on them to prevent burning.
- Experiment with different seasonings and herbs to create unique flavor combinations.
- To make kale chips, simply replace the root vegetables with 2-3 cups of curly kale leaves, stems removed and discarded, and leaves torn into bite-sized pieces.

Air Fryer Popcorn

Serving Size: 2-4 cups (about 2-4 servings)

Prep Time: 2 minutes

Cooking Time: 5-7 minutes

Total Time: 7-9 minutes

Nutrition Information (per serving):

- Calories: 100
- Fat: 2g
- Saturated Fat: 0g
- Cholesterol: 0mg
- Sodium: 5mg
- Carbohydrates: 20g
- Fiber: 2g
- Sugar: 0g
- Protein: 2g

Ingredients:

- 1/4 cup popcorn kernels
- 1 tablespoon oil (such as canola or avocado oil)
- Salt to taste (optional)

Directions:

1. Preheat the air fryer: Set the air fryer to 375°F (190°C).
2. Mix the popcorn kernels and oil: In a bowl, mix together the popcorn kernels and oil until the kernels are evenly coated.
3. Add the popcorn kernels to the air fryer: Pour the popcorn kernels into the air fryer basket. You may need to cook them in batches depending on the size of your air fryer.
4. Cook the popcorn: Cook the popcorn for 5-7 minutes, shaking the basket halfway through. You may hear the popping sounds slow down, which indicates that the popcorn is done.
5. Season with salt (optional): Once the popcorn is cooked, sprinkle salt to taste if desired.
6. Serve: Serve the air fryer popcorn hot and enjoy!

Tips:

- Use the right type of popcorn kernels: Look for kernels specifically labeled as "air popper" or "microwave" kernels.
- Don't overcrowd the air fryer basket: Cook the popcorn in batches if necessary, to ensure even cooking.
- Experiment with seasonings: Try adding different seasonings, such as grated Parmesan cheese, paprika, or chili powder, to give your air fryer popcorn a unique flavor.

Stuffed Jalapeños

Serving Size: 12-15 peppers (about 4-6 servings)

Prep Time: 20 minutes

Cooking Time: 15-20 minutes

Total Time: 35-40 minutes

Nutrition Information (per serving):

- Calories: 120
- Fat: 9g
- Saturated Fat: 3.5g
- Cholesterol: 20mg
- Sodium: 150mg
- Carbohydrates: 6g
- Fiber: 1g

- Sugar: 1g
- Protein: 4g

Ingredients:

- 12-15 large jalapeño peppers
- 1 cup cream cheese, softened
- 1/2 cup shredded cheddar cheese
- 1/4 cup chopped cilantro
- 1/4 cup chopped scallions (green onions)
- 1/2 teaspoon garlic powder
- Salt and pepper, to taste
- 1 egg, beaten (for egg wash)
- 1 cup panko breadcrumbs (optional)

Directions:

1. Preheat the oven: Preheat the oven to 375°F (190°C).
2. Prepare the jalapeños: Cut off the stems of the jalapeños and carefully scoop out the seeds and membranes. Rinse the peppers under cold water to remove any remaining seeds or spiciness.
3. Prepare the filling: In a bowl, mix together the cream cheese, cheddar cheese, cilantro, scallions, garlic powder, salt, and pepper until well combined.
4. Stuff the jalapeños: Stuff each jalapeño pepper with the cream cheese mixture, filling them as full as possible.
5. Dip in egg wash and breadcrumbs (optional): If desired, dip the stuffed jalapeños in the beaten egg and then roll them in panko breadcrumbs to coat.
6. Bake the jalapeños: Place the stuffed jalapeños on a baking sheet lined with parchment paper. Bake for 15-20 minutes, or until the peppers are tender and the filling is heated through.
7. Serve: Serve the spicy stuffed jalapeños hot and enjoy!

Tips:

- Use gloves when handling jalapeños to avoid irritating your skin.
- Adjust the level of heat in the filling by using more or less jalapeño peppers.
- Experiment with different types of cheese or add some diced ham or bacon to the filling for added flavor.

Garlic Parmesan Knots

Serving Size: 8-10 knots (about 4-6 servings)

Prep Time: 20 minutes

Cooking Time: 12-15 minutes

Total Time: 32-35 minutes

Nutrition Information (per serving):

- Calories: 220
- Fat: 8g
- Saturated Fat: 2g
- Cholesterol: 10mg
- Sodium: 350mg
- Carbohydrates: 30g
- Fiber: 1g
- Sugar: 1g
- Protein: 5g

Ingredients:

- 1 1/2 cups warm water
- 2 teaspoons active dry yeast
- 3 tablespoons olive oil
- 1 teaspoon salt
- 3 cups all-purpose flour
- 1/2 cup grated Parmesan cheese
- 2 cloves garlic, minced
- 1 egg, beaten (for egg wash)
- Fresh parsley, chopped (optional)

Directions:

1. Activate the yeast: In a large bowl, combine the warm water and yeast. Let it sit for 5-7 minutes, until the yeast is activated and foamy.
2. Mix the dough: Add the olive oil, salt, and 2 cups of flour to the bowl. Mix until a shaggy dough forms. Gradually add the remaining cup of flour, until the dough becomes smooth and elastic.
3. Knead the dough: Knead the dough on a floured surface for 5-7 minutes, until it becomes smooth and elastic.

4. Let the dough rise: Place the dough in a greased bowl, cover it with a damp cloth, and let it rise in a warm place for 1 hour, until it has doubled in size.
5. Prepare the garlic butter: Mix the minced garlic and grated Parmesan cheese in a small bowl.
6. Shape the knots: Divide the dough into 8-10 equal pieces. Roll each piece into a rope and tie it into a knot. Place the knots onto a baking sheet lined with parchment paper.
7. Brush with egg wash and garlic butter: Brush the tops of the knots with the beaten egg and then sprinkle with the garlic butter mixture.
8. Bake the knots: Bake the knots in a preheated oven at 375°F (190°C) for 12-15 minutes, until golden brown.
9. Serve: Serve the garlic Parmesan knots warm, garnished with chopped fresh parsley if desired.

Tips:

- To make ahead, prepare the dough and let it rise. Then, shape the knots and refrigerate or freeze them until ready to bake.
- Experiment with different herbs and spices, such as dried oregano or red pepper flakes, to add extra flavor to the knots.
- Serve the garlic Parmesan knots as a side dish or use them as a base for sliders or sandwiches.

Chapter 4

Main Courses

Juicy Air Fryer Chicken

Serving Size: 4-6 servings (about 2-3 lbs chicken)

Prep Time: 10 minutes

Cooking Time: 20-25 minutes

Total Time: 30-35 minutes

Nutrition Information (per serving):

- Calories: 260
- Fat: 8g
- Saturated Fat: 2g
- Cholesterol: 80mg
- Sodium: 250mg
- Carbohydrates: 0g
- Fiber: 0g
- Sugar: 0g
- Protein: 35g

Ingredients:

- 2-3 lbs boneless, skinless chicken breasts or thighs
- 2 tbsp olive oil
- 1 tsp salt
- 1 tsp pepper
- 1 tsp garlic powder
- 1 tsp paprika
- 1 tsp dried thyme
- 1/4 tsp cayenne pepper (optional)

Directions:

1. Preheat the air fryer: Preheat the air fryer to 400°F (200°C).
2. Prep the chicken: Rinse the chicken and pat it dry with paper towels.

3. Season the chicken: In a small bowl, mix together the olive oil, salt, pepper, garlic powder, paprika, thyme, and cayenne pepper (if using). Rub the mixture all over the chicken, making sure to coat it evenly.

4. Cook the chicken: Place the chicken in the air fryer basket, leaving some space between each piece. Cook the chicken for 20-25 minutes, or until it reaches an internal temperature of 165°F (74°C).

5. Flip and shake: Halfway through cooking, flip the chicken and shake the basket to ensure even cooking.

6. Check the temperature: Use a meat thermometer to check the internal temperature of the chicken.

7. Let it rest: Once the chicken is cooked, remove it from the air fryer and let it rest for 5-10 minutes before slicing and serving.

Tips:

- Make sure to not overcrowd the air fryer basket, as this can affect the cooking performance.
- If you prefer a crisper exterior, you can increase the cooking temperature to 420°F (220°C) for the last 5 minutes of cooking.
- Experiment with different seasonings and marinades to add extra flavor to your air fryer chicken.

Beef and Pork Recipes

Serving Size: 20-25 meatballs (about 4-6 servings)

Prep Time: 20 minutes

Cooking Time: 18-20 minutes

Total Time: 38-40 minutes

Nutrition Information (per serving):

- Calories: 320
- Fat: 22g
- Saturated Fat: 8g
- Cholesterol: 60mg
- Sodium: 350mg
- Carbohydrates: 10g
- Fiber: 1g
- Sugar: 1g
- Protein: 25g

Ingredients:

- 1 lb ground beef
- 1/2 lb ground pork
- 1/2 cup breadcrumbs
- 1 egg
- 1/4 cup grated Parmesan cheese
- 1/4 cup chopped fresh parsley
- 2 cloves garlic, minced
- 1 tsp dried oregano
- Salt and pepper, to taste
- Olive oil, for cooking

Directions:

1. Preheat the oven: Preheat the oven to 400°F (200°C).
2. Prepare the meat mixture: In a large bowl, combine the ground beef, ground pork, breadcrumbs, egg, Parmesan cheese, parsley, garlic, oregano, salt, and pepper. Mix everything together with your hands or a wooden spoon until just combined. Be careful not to overmix.
3. Form the meatballs: Use your hands to shape the meat mixture into meatballs, about 1 1/2 inches (3.8 cm) in diameter. You should end up with around 20-25 meatballs.
4. Cook the meatballs: Place the meatballs on a baking sheet lined with parchment paper, leaving a little space between each meatball to allow for even cooking. Drizzle with a little olive oil. Bake the meatballs in the preheated oven for 18-20 minutes, or until cooked through and lightly browned on the outside.
5. Serve: Serve the beef and pork meatballs hot, garnished with some extra parsley if desired. You can serve them as is, or with your favorite marinara sauce and pasta.

Tips:

- Make sure to handle the meat mixture gently to avoid compacting it too much, which can make the meatballs dense and heavy.
- If you want to make the meatballs more substantial, you can add some chopped onions, carrots, or zucchini to the meat mixture.
- Experiment with different seasonings and herbs to give the meatballs a unique flavor profile.

Seafood Specialties

Serving Size: 4-6 servings

Prep Time: 15 minutes

Cooking Time: 10-12 minutes

Total Time: 25-27 minutes

Nutrition Information (per serving):

- Calories: 240
- Fat: 12g
- Saturated Fat: 6g
- Cholesterol: 120mg
- Sodium: 350mg
- Carbohydrates: 4g
- Fiber: 0g
- Sugar: 0g
- Protein: 26g

Ingredients:

- 1 pound large shrimp, peeled and deveined
- 1 pound large scallops
- 4 cloves garlic, minced
- 2 tablespoons unsalted butter
- 1 tablespoon freshly squeezed lemon juice
- 1 teaspoon dried parsley
- Salt and pepper, to taste
- Fresh parsley, chopped (optional)

Directions:

1. Rinse and pat dry the seafood: Rinse the shrimp and scallops under cold water and pat them dry with paper towels.
2. Melt the butter: In a large skillet, melt the butter over medium-high heat.
3. Add the garlic: Add the minced garlic to the melted butter and sauté for 1-2 minutes, until fragrant.
4. Add the shrimp and scallops: Add the shrimp and scallops to the skillet and sauté for 2-3 minutes per side, until they are cooked through and slightly browned.
5. Add the lemon juice and parsley: Squeeze the fresh lemon juice over the seafood and sprinkle with dried parsley.

6. Season with salt and pepper: Season the seafood with salt and pepper to taste.
7. Serve: Serve the garlic butter shrimp and scallops hot, garnished with chopped fresh parsley if desired.

Tips:

- Make sure to not overcook the seafood, as it can become tough and rubbery.
- Use fresh and high-quality ingredients to ensure the best flavor and texture.
- Experiment with different seasonings and marinades to add extra flavor to your seafood dish.

Variations:

- Add some diced onions, bell peppers, or mushrooms to the skillet with the garlic for added flavor and nutrients.
- Use different types of seafood, such as lobster or crab, for a more luxurious dish.
- Serve the garlic butter shrimp and scallops with a side of rice, pasta, or roasted vegetables for a complete meal.

Vegetarian Options

Serving Size: 4-6 servings

Prep Time: 20 minutes

Cooking Time: 30-40 minutes

Total Time: 50-60 minutes

Nutrition Information (per serving):

- Calories: 420
- Fat: 10g
- Saturated Fat: 1.5g
- Cholesterol: 0mg
- Sodium: 200mg
- Carbohydrates: 60g
- Fiber: 8g
- Sugar: 8g
- Protein: 15g

Ingredients:

- 1 cup quinoa, rinsed and drained
- 2 cups water or vegetable broth
- 2 tablespoons olive oil
- 1 large sweet potato, peeled and cubed
- 1 large red bell pepper, seeded and cubed
- 1 large zucchini, sliced
- 1 cup cherry tomatoes, halved
- 1 small red onion, thinly sliced
- 2 cloves garlic, minced
- 1 teaspoon dried thyme
- Salt and pepper, to taste
- Optional: avocado, feta cheese, or nuts for topping

Directions:

1. Preheat the oven: Preheat the oven to 400°F (200°C).
2. Cook the quinoa: In a medium saucepan, bring the quinoa and water or broth to a boil. Reduce the heat to low, cover, and simmer for 15-20 minutes, until the quinoa is tender and fluffy.
3. Roast the vegetables: In a large bowl, toss the sweet potato, bell pepper, zucchini, cherry tomatoes, and red onion with the olive oil, garlic, and thyme. Season with salt and pepper to taste. Spread the vegetables in a single layer on a large baking sheet. Roast in the preheated oven for 25-30 minutes, until the vegetables are tender and lightly browned.
4. Assemble the bowls: Divide the cooked quinoa among four to six bowls. Top with the roasted vegetables and any desired toppings, such as avocado, feta cheese, or nuts.
5. Serve: Serve the roasted vegetable quinoa bowls hot, garnished with fresh herbs or a squeeze of lemon juice, if desired.

Tips:

- Customize the recipe with your favorite vegetables or add some protein sources, such as tofu or tempeh, for added nutrition.
- Use different seasonings or spices, such as cumin or smoked paprika, to give the dish a unique flavor profile.
- Make the recipe ahead of time and refrigerate or freeze it for a quick and easy meal.

Air Fryer Burgers

Serving Size: 4-6 burgers

Prep Time: 10 minutes

Cooking Time: 8-12 minutes

Total Time: 18-22 minutes

Nutrition Information (per serving):

- Calories: 320
- Fat: 12g
- Saturated Fat: 4g
- Cholesterol: 60mg
- Sodium: 350mg
- Carbohydrates: 20g
- Fiber: 0g
- Sugar: 0g
- Protein: 25g

Ingredients:

- 1 pound ground beef (80/20 or 70/30 lean to fat ratio works best)
- 1/2 medium onion, finely chopped
- 2 cloves garlic, minced
- 1 tablespoon Worcestershire sauce
- 1 teaspoon salt
- 1/2 teaspoon black pepper
- 1/4 teaspoon paprika
- 4-6 hamburger buns
- Lettuce, tomato, cheese, pickles, and any other desired toppings

Directions:

1. Preheat the air fryer: Preheat the air fryer to 375°F (190°C).
2. Prepare the burger mixture: In a large bowl, combine the ground beef, chopped onion, minced garlic, Worcestershire sauce, salt, black pepper, and paprika. Use your hands or a spoon to mix the ingredients until just combined. Do not overmix.
3. Form the patties: Divide the burger mixture into 4-6 equal portions, depending on the desired patty size. Shape each portion into a ball and then flatten it slightly into a patty.

4. Cook the patties: Place the patties in the air fryer basket, leaving some space between each patty. Cook the patties for 8-12 minutes, or until they reach your desired level of doneness. Flip the patties halfway through cooking.

5. Assemble the burgers: Once the patties are cooked, assemble the burgers by spreading a slice of cheese on the bottom bun, followed by a cooked patty, lettuce, tomato, pickles, and any other desired toppings. Top with the top bun.

6. Serve and enjoy: Serve the juicy air fryer burgers hot and enjoy!

Tips:

- Make sure to not overcrowd the air fryer basket, as this can affect the cooking performance.
- Use a thermometer to ensure the patties reach a safe internal temperature of at least 160°F (71°C).
- Experiment with different seasonings and toppings to create unique burger flavors.

Crispy Air Fryer Tofu

Serving Size: 4-6 servings

Prep Time: 10 minutes

Cooking Time: 12-15 minutes

Total Time: 22-25 minutes

Nutrition Information (per serving):

- Calories: 200
- Fat: 10g
- Saturated Fat: 1.5g
- Cholesterol: 0mg
- Sodium: 200mg
- Carbohydrates: 10g
- Fiber: 2g
- Sugar: 0g
- Protein: 20g

Ingredients:

- 1 block firm or extra-firm tofu, drained and cut into bite-sized cubes
- 1/2 cup cornstarch
- 1/2 teaspoon salt

- 1/4 teaspoon black pepper
- 1/4 teaspoon garlic powder
- 1/4 teaspoon paprika
- 2 tablespoons olive oil
- Optional: Additional seasonings or herbs, such as dried thyme or cumin

Directions:

1. Preheat the air fryer: Preheat the air fryer to 400°F (200°C).
2. Prepare the tofu: Cut the tofu into bite-sized cubes and wrap them in a clean kitchen towel or paper towels. Gently press the tofu to remove excess moisture.
3. Coat the tofu with cornstarch mixture: In a shallow dish, mix together the cornstarch, salt, black pepper, garlic powder, and paprika. Toss the tofu cubes in the cornstarch mixture to coat evenly.
4. Cook the tofu: Place the coated tofu cubes in the air fryer basket, leaving some space between each cube. Cook the tofu for 12-15 minutes, or until it is crispy and golden brown. Shake the basket halfway through cooking.
5. Drizzle with olive oil: Remove the tofu from the air fryer and drizzle with olive oil.
6. Serve: Serve the crispy air fryer tofu hot, garnished with chopped fresh herbs or scallions, if desired.

Tips:

- Use firm or extra-firm tofu for the best results, as it will hold its shape better during cooking.
- Adjust the cooking time based on the size of your tofu cubes and your desired level of crispiness.
- Experiment with different seasonings and herbs to add unique flavors to your crispy air fryer tofu.

Comfort Food Classics

Serving Size: 6-8 servings

Prep Time: 20 minutes

Cooking Time: 25-30 minutes

Total Time: 45-50 minutes

Nutrition Information (per serving):

- Calories: 420
- Fat: 24g
- Saturated Fat: 14g

- Cholesterol: 60mg
- Sodium: 400mg
- Carbohydrates: 30g
- Fiber: 2g
- Sugar: 5g
- Protein: 20g

Ingredients:

- 8 oz macaroni
- 2 cups milk
- 2 cups grated cheddar cheese
- 1 cup grated mozzarella cheese
- 1/4 cup all-purpose flour
- 1/2 teaspoon salt
- 1/4 teaspoon black pepper
- 2 tablespoons butter
- Optional: breadcrumbs and chopped herbs for topping

Directions:

1. Preheat the oven: Preheat the oven to 375°F (190°C).
2. Cook the macaroni: Bring a large pot of salted water to a boil. Cook the macaroni according to the package instructions until al dente. Drain and set aside.
3. Make the cheese sauce: In a medium saucepan, melt the butter over medium heat. Add the flour and whisk together to make a roux, cooking for 1-2 minutes. Slowly pour in the milk, whisking constantly to avoid lumps. Bring the mixture to a simmer and cook until it thickens, stirring occasionally. Remove from heat and stir in the cheddar and mozzarella cheese until melted and smooth. Season with salt and pepper to taste.
4. Assemble the mac and cheese: In a large mixing bowl, combine the cooked macaroni and cheese sauce. Stir until the macaroni is well coated.
5. Transfer to a baking dish: Transfer the mac and cheese to a 9x13 inch baking dish.
6. Top with additional cheese and breadcrumbs (optional): If desired, sprinkle additional grated cheese and breadcrumbs on top of the mac and cheese.
7. Bake until golden brown: Bake the mac and cheese in the preheated oven for 25-30 minutes, until the top is golden brown and the mac and cheese is heated through.
8. Serve and enjoy: Serve the creamy mac and cheese hot, garnished with chopped herbs if desired.

Tips:

- Use a variety of cheeses, such as Gruyère or Parmesan, to add depth and complexity to the dish.
- Add some spice with a pinch of cayenne pepper or red pepper flakes.
- Experiment with different pasta shapes, such as shells or elbows, for a change of pace.

Chapter 5

Side Dishes

Roasted Vegetables

Serving Size: 4-6 servings

Prep Time: 15 minutes

Cooking Time: 25-30 minutes

Total Time: 40-45 minutes

Nutrition Information (per serving):

- Calories: 120
- Fat: 2g
- Saturated Fat: 0g
- Cholesterol: 0mg
- Sodium: 50mg
- Carbohydrates: 25g
- Fiber: 5g
- Sugar: 8g
- Protein: 3g

Ingredients:

- 2 large carrots, peeled and chopped
- 2 large Brussels sprouts, trimmed and halved
- 2 large red bell peppers, seeded and chopped
- 2 large sweet potatoes, peeled and chopped
- 2 cloves garlic, minced
- 2 tablespoons olive oil
- Salt and pepper, to taste
- Optional: other vegetables such as broccoli, cauliflower, or zucchini

Directions:

1. Preheat the oven: Preheat the oven to 425°F (220°C).

2. Toss the vegetables with oil and seasonings: In a large bowl, toss the chopped carrots, Brussels sprouts, bell peppers, and sweet potatoes with the olive oil, garlic, salt, and pepper until they are evenly coated.

3. Spread the vegetables on a baking sheet: Spread the vegetables in a single layer on a large baking sheet.

4. Roast the vegetables: Roast the vegetables in the preheated oven for 25-30 minutes, or until they are tender and lightly browned.

5. Serve: Serve the roasted vegetable medley hot, garnished with chopped fresh herbs if desired.

Tips:

- Use a variety of colorful vegetables to make the dish visually appealing.
- Adjust the cooking time based on the tenderness of the vegetables.
- Experiment with different seasonings and herbs, such as dried thyme or rosemary, to add unique flavors to the dish.

Variations:

- Add some protein to the dish by tossing cooked chicken, tofu, or chickpeas with the vegetables.
- Use different cooking methods, such as grilling or sautéing, to change the texture and flavor of the vegetables.
- Make the dish more substantial by serving the roasted vegetables over quinoa, brown rice, or whole grain bread.

Garlic Parmesan Potatoes

Serving Size: 4-6 servings

Prep Time: 15 minutes

Cooking Time: 20-25 minutes

Total Time: 35-40 minutes

Nutrition Information (per serving):

- Calories: 220
- Fat: 9g
- Saturated Fat: 2.5g
- Cholesterol: 10mg
- Sodium: 250mg

- Carbohydrates: 30g
- Fiber: 2g
- Sugar: 1g
- Protein: 4g

Ingredients:

- 2-3 large potatoes, peeled and cut into 1-inch wedges
- 2 cloves garlic, minced
- 1/2 cup grated Parmesan cheese
- 1/4 cup olive oil
- 1 teaspoon dried thyme
- Salt and pepper, to taste
- Optional: chopped fresh parsley or chives for garnish

Directions:

1. Preheat the oven: Preheat the oven to 425°F (220°C).
2. Prepare the potatoes: Cut the potatoes into 1-inch wedges and place them in a large bowl.
3. Mix the garlic and Parmesan cheese: In a small bowl, mix together the minced garlic and grated Parmesan cheese.
4. Toss the potatoes with oil and seasonings: Add the olive oil, thyme, salt, and pepper to the bowl with the potatoes. Toss to coat the potatoes evenly.
5. Sprinkle with garlic and Parmesan cheese: Sprinkle the garlic and Parmesan cheese mixture over the potatoes and toss again to coat.
6. Bake the potatoes: Spread the potatoes out in a single layer on a large baking sheet. Bake in the preheated oven for 20-25 minutes, or until the potatoes are tender and golden brown.
7. Serve: Serve the garlic Parmesan potatoes hot, garnished with chopped fresh parsley or chives if desired.

Tips:

- Use high-quality Parmesan cheese for the best flavor.
- Adjust the amount of garlic to your taste.
- Experiment with different herbs, such as rosemary or oregano, to add unique flavors to the potatoes.

Variations:

- Add some spice with a pinch of red pepper flakes.
- Use different types of potatoes, such as sweet potatoes or Yukon golds, for a change of pace.
- Make the dish more substantial by serving the garlic Parmesan potatoes as a side dish with grilled chicken or steak.

Stuffed Mushrooms

Serving Size: 12-15 mushrooms (about 4-6 servings)

Prep Time: 15 minutes

Cooking Time: 15-20 minutes

Total Time: 30-35 minutes

Nutrition Information (per serving):

- Calories: 120
- Fat: 7g
- Saturated Fat: 1g
- Cholesterol: 10mg
- Sodium: 200mg
- Carbohydrates: 10g
- Fiber: 1g
- Sugar: 2g
- Protein: 4g

Ingredients:

- 12-15 large mushrooms (such as portobello or cremini), cleaned and stems removed
- 1/2 cup breadcrumbs
- 1/2 cup grated cheddar cheese
- 1/4 cup chopped onion
- 2 cloves garlic, minced
- 1 tablespoon olive oil
- 1 teaspoon dried thyme
- Salt and pepper, to taste
- Optional: chopped fresh parsley or chives for garnish

Directions:

1. Preheat the oven: Preheat the oven to 375°F (190°C).
2. Prepare the mushroom caps: Remove the stems from the mushrooms and scoop out the insides to create a shell. Finely chop the removed mushroom insides and set aside.
3. Mix the filling ingredients: In a medium bowl, combine the breadcrumbs, cheddar cheese, chopped onion, garlic, olive oil, thyme, salt, and pepper. Mix well.
4. Add the chopped mushroom insides: Add the chopped mushroom insides to the filling mixture and mix until well combined.

5. Stuff the mushroom caps: Divide the filling mixture among the mushroom caps, spooning it into the caps and mounding it slightly.

6. Bake the stuffed mushrooms: Place the stuffed mushrooms on a baking sheet lined with parchment paper and bake in the preheated oven for 15-20 minutes, or until the mushrooms are tender and the filling is golden brown.

7. Serve: Serve the savory stuffed mushrooms hot, garnished with chopped fresh parsley or chives if desired.

Tips:

- Use a variety of cheeses, such as Parmesan or feta, to add unique flavors to the filling.
- Add some heat with a pinch of red pepper flakes.
- Experiment with different herbs, such as rosemary or oregano, to add depth to the filling.

Variations:

- Use different types of mushrooms, such as shiitake or oyster mushrooms, for a change of pace.
- Add some crunch with chopped nuts or seeds.
- Make the dish more substantial by serving the stuffed mushrooms as a main course with a side salad or roasted vegetables.

Air Fryer Rice

Serving Size: 4-6 servings

Prep Time: 10 minutes

Cooking Time: 10-12 minutes

Total Time: 20-22 minutes

Nutrition Information (per serving):

- Calories: 250
- Fat: 8g
- Saturated Fat: 1g
- Cholesterol: 10mg
- Sodium: 200mg
- Carbohydrates: 35g
- Fiber: 2g

- Sugar: 1g
- Protein: 5g

Ingredients:

- 2 cups cooked rice (preferably day-old rice)
- 1 tablespoon vegetable oil
- 1 small onion, diced
- 2 cloves garlic, minced
- 1 cup mixed vegetables (e.g., peas, carrots, corn)
- 2 eggs, beaten
- 1 teaspoon soy sauce
- Salt and pepper, to taste
- Optional: scallions, chopped nuts, or diced cooked chicken for added flavor and texture

Directions:

1. Preheat the air fryer: Preheat the air fryer to 375°F (190°C).
2. Heat the oil and cook the onion and garlic: In the air fryer basket, heat the vegetable oil over medium-high heat. Add the diced onion and minced garlic and cook until the onion is translucent.
3. Add the mixed vegetables and cooked rice: Add the mixed vegetables and cooked rice to the air fryer basket. Stir-fry for 2-3 minutes, breaking up any clumps with a spatula.
4. Push the rice mixture to one side: Push the rice mixture to one side of the air fryer basket.
5. Add the beaten eggs: Pour the beaten eggs into the empty side of the air fryer basket. Scramble the eggs until cooked through, breaking them up into small pieces as they cook.
6. Mix the eggs with the rice mixture: Mix the scrambled eggs with the rice mixture.
7. Add the soy sauce and season with salt and pepper: Add the soy sauce and season with salt and pepper to taste.
8. Serve: Serve the air fryer fried rice hot, garnished with chopped scallions, nuts, or diced cooked chicken if desired.

Tips:

- Use day-old rice to make the best air fryer fried rice.
- Customize the recipe by adding your favorite vegetables, meat, or seasonings.
- Experiment with different cooking times and temperatures to achieve the perfect texture and crispiness.

Crispy Brussels Sprouts

Serving Size: 4-6 servings

Prep Time: 10 minutes

Cooking Time: 20-25 minutes

Total Time: 30-35 minutes

Nutrition Information (per serving):

- Calories: 120
- Fat: 7g
- Saturated Fat: 1g
- Cholesterol: 0mg
- Sodium: 200mg
- Carbohydrates: 15g
- Fiber: 5g
- Sugar: 5g
- Protein: 4g

Ingredients:

- 1 pound Brussels sprouts, trimmed and halved
- 2 cloves garlic, minced
- 2 tablespoons olive oil
- 1 tablespoon freshly squeezed lemon juice
- 1 teaspoon salt
- 1/2 teaspoon black pepper
- 1/4 teaspoon red pepper flakes (optional)
- 1/4 cup grated Parmesan cheese (optional)

Directions:

1. Preheat the oven: Preheat the oven to 400°F (200°C).
2. Toss the Brussels sprouts with oil and seasonings: In a large bowl, toss the Brussels sprouts with the olive oil, garlic, salt, black pepper, and red pepper flakes (if using) until they are evenly coated.
3. Spread the Brussels sprouts on a baking sheet: Spread the Brussels sprouts in a single layer on a large baking sheet.
4. Roast the Brussels sprouts: Roast the Brussels sprouts in the preheated oven for 20-25 minutes, or until they are tender and caramelized, stirring occasionally.

5. Add the lemon juice and Parmesan cheese (if using): After the Brussels sprouts have roasted for 20-25 minutes, remove them from the oven and sprinkle with the freshly squeezed lemon juice and grated Parmesan cheese (if using). Toss to coat.
6. Serve: Serve the crispy Brussels sprouts hot, garnished with chopped fresh herbs or lemon wedges if desired.

Tips:

- Cut the Brussels sprouts in half or quarters to help them roast more evenly.
- Use a high-quality olive oil to add depth and richness to the dish.
- Experiment with different seasonings and toppings, such as chopped bacon or balsamic glaze, to add unique flavors to the Brussels sprouts.

Variations:

- Add some crunch with chopped nuts or seeds.
- Use different types of citrus, such as lime or orange, for a different flavor profile.
- Make the dish more substantial by serving the crispy Brussels sprouts as a side dish with roasted chicken or pork.

Cheesy Cauliflower Bites

Serving Size: 12-15 bites (about 4-6 servings)

Prep Time: 15 minutes

Cooking Time: 15-20 minutes

Total Time: 30-35 minutes

Nutrition Information (per serving):

- Calories: 150
- Fat: 9g
- Saturated Fat: 4g
- Cholesterol: 20mg
- Sodium: 200mg
- Carbohydrates: 10g
- Fiber: 5g
- Sugar: 5g
- Protein: 6g

Ingredients:

- 1 head of cauliflower, broken into florets
- 1 cup grated cheddar cheese
- 1/2 cup grated mozzarella cheese
- 1/4 cup all-purpose flour
- 1/2 teaspoon paprika
- 1/2 teaspoon garlic powder
- 1/2 teaspoon salt
- 1/4 teaspoon black pepper
- 2 tablespoons olive oil
- Optional: chopped fresh parsley or chives for garnish

Directions:

1. Preheat the oven: Preheat the oven to 400°F (200°C).
2. Prepare the cauliflower: Pulse the cauliflower florets in a food processor until they resemble rice.
3. Mix the cheese and flour mixture: In a medium bowl, mix together the grated cheddar cheese, mozzarella cheese, flour, paprika, garlic powder, salt, and black pepper.
4. Add the cauliflower to the cheese mixture: Add the pulsed cauliflower to the cheese mixture and stir until well combined.
5. Form the cauliflower bites: Using your hands, shape the cauliflower mixture into small balls, about 1 1/2 inches in diameter. You should end up with around 12-15 bites.
6. Drizzle with olive oil: Place the cauliflower bites on a baking sheet lined with parchment paper and drizzle with olive oil.
7. Bake until golden brown: Bake the cauliflower bites in the preheated oven for 15-20 minutes, or until they are golden brown and crispy on the outside.
8. Serve: Serve the cheesy cauliflower bites hot, garnished with chopped fresh parsley or chives if desired.

Tips:

- Use a variety of cheeses, such as Parmesan or feta, to add unique flavors to the cauliflower bites.
- Experiment with different seasonings, such as dried thyme or oregano, to add depth to the dish.
- Make the cauliflower bites ahead of time and refrigerate or freeze them for a quick and easy snack.

Air Fryer Corn on the Cob

Serving Size: 4-6 servings

Prep Time: 5 minutes

Cooking Time: 10-12 minutes

Total Time: 15-17 minutes

Nutrition Information (per serving):

- Calories: 80
- Fat: 1g
- Saturated Fat: 0g
- Cholesterol: 0mg
- Sodium: 10mg
- Carbohydrates: 18g
- Fiber: 2g
- Sugar: 6g
- Protein: 2g

Ingredients:

- 4-6 ears of corn, husked and silked
- 1 tablespoon olive oil
- Salt and pepper, to taste
- Optional: garlic powder, paprika, or other seasonings of your choice

Directions:

1. Preheat the air fryer: Preheat the air fryer to 375°F (190°C).
2. Brush the corn with oil and season: Brush the corn with olive oil and sprinkle with salt, pepper, and any desired seasonings.
3. Place the corn in the air fryer basket: Place the corn in the air fryer basket, leaving some space between each ear.
4. Cook the corn: Cook the corn in the preheated air fryer for 10-12 minutes, or until it is tender and lightly browned, turning occasionally.
5. Serve: Serve the air fryer corn on the cob hot, slathered with butter, mayonnaise, or your favorite toppings.

Tips:

- Use fresh corn for the best flavor and texture.
- Adjust the cooking time based on the size and type of corn you use.
- Experiment with different seasonings and toppings to add unique flavors to your air fryer corn on the cob.

Variations:

- Add some smokiness with a sprinkle of smoked paprika.
- Use different types of oil, such as avocado oil or grapeseed oil, for a unique flavor.
- Make the dish more substantial by serving the air fryer corn on the cob as a side dish with grilled meats or vegetables.

Chapter 6

Healthy Choices

Low-Calorie Recipes

Serving Size: 4 servings

Prep Time: 10 minutes

Cooking Time: 15 minutes

Total Time: 25 minutes

Nutrition Information (per serving):

- Calories: 220
- Fat: 8g
- Saturated Fat: 1.5g
- Cholesterol: 60mg
- Sodium: 200mg
- Carbohydrates: 15g
- Fiber: 5g
- Sugar: 5g
- Protein: 25g

Ingredients:

- 1 pound boneless, skinless chicken breast, cut into bite-sized pieces
- 2 cups mixed vegetables (such as broccoli, bell peppers, carrots, and snap peas)
- 2 tablespoons olive oil
- 1 tablespoon soy sauce
- 1 tablespoon honey
- 1 teaspoon grated ginger
- Salt and pepper, to taste
- Optional: sesame seeds and chopped green onions for garnish

Directions:

1. Heat the oil in a skillet: Heat the olive oil in a large skillet or wok over medium-high heat.
2. Cook the chicken: Add the chicken to the skillet and cook until browned and cooked through, about 5-7 minutes. Remove from the skillet and set aside.

3. Cook the vegetables: Add the mixed vegetables to the skillet and cook until tender-crisp, about 3-5 minutes.
4. Make the sauce: In a small bowl, whisk together the soy sauce, honey, and grated ginger.
5. Combine the chicken and vegetables with the sauce: Add the cooked chicken back into the skillet with the vegetables and pour the sauce over the top. Stir to combine.
6. Season with salt and pepper: Season with salt and pepper to taste.
7. Serve: Serve the low-calorie chicken and vegetable stir-fry hot, garnished with sesame seeds and chopped green onions if desired.

Tips:

- Use a variety of colorful vegetables to add visual appeal and nutrients to the dish.
- Substitute the chicken with tofu or shrimp for a different protein option.
- Experiment with different seasonings and spices, such as cumin or chili flakes, to add unique flavors to the dish.

Variations:

- Add some crunch with chopped nuts or seeds.
- Use different types of oil, such as avocado oil or grapeseed oil, for a unique flavor.
- Make the dish more substantial by serving the low-calorie chicken and vegetable stir-fry with brown rice or whole grain noodles.

Keto-Friendly Meals

Serving Size: 4 servings

Prep Time: 10 minutes

Cooking Time: 12-15 minutes

Total Time: 22-25 minutes

Nutrition Information (per serving):

- Calories: 360
- Fat: 26g
- Saturated Fat: 4g
- Cholesterol: 60mg
- Sodium: 200mg

- Carbohydrates: 5g
- Fiber: 0g
- Sugar: 0g
- Protein: 35g

Ingredients:

- 4 salmon fillets (6 ounces each)
- 1/4 cup freshly squeezed lemon juice
- 2 cloves garlic, minced
- 1 tablespoon chopped fresh rosemary
- 1 tablespoon chopped fresh thyme
- 1/2 teaspoon salt
- 1/4 teaspoon black pepper
- 2 tablespoons olive oil

Directions:

1. Preheat the oven: Preheat the oven to 400°F (200°C).
2. Prepare the salmon: Line a baking sheet with parchment paper or aluminum foil. Place the salmon fillets on the prepared baking sheet.
3. Mix the lemon juice and herbs: In a small bowl, mix together the lemon juice, garlic, rosemary, thyme, salt, and pepper.
4. Brush the salmon with the lemon mixture: Brush the lemon mixture evenly over the salmon fillets.
5. Drizzle with olive oil: Drizzle the olive oil over the salmon fillets.
6. Bake the salmon: Bake the salmon in the preheated oven for 12-15 minutes, or until cooked through.
7. Serve: Serve the keto-friendly baked salmon hot, garnished with chopped fresh herbs if desired.

Tips:

- Use wild-caught salmon for the best flavor and nutrition.
- Adjust the cooking time based on the thickness of the salmon fillets.
- Experiment with different herbs and seasonings to add unique flavors to the dish.

Variations:

- Add some heat with a pinch of red pepper flakes.
- Use different types of fish, such as tilapia or cod, for a change of pace.
- Make the dish more substantial by serving the baked salmon with a side of roasted vegetables or a keto-friendly salad.

Gluten-Free Options

Serving Size: 4-6 servings

Prep Time: 15 minutes

Cooking Time: 20-25 minutes

Total Time: 35-40 minutes

Nutrition Information (per serving):

- Calories: 420
- Fat: 10g
- Saturated Fat: 1.5g
- Cholesterol: 0mg
- Sodium: 200mg
- Carbohydrates: 60g
- Fiber: 10g
- Sugar: 5g
- Protein: 15g

Ingredients:

- 1 cup quinoa, rinsed and drained
- 2 cups water or vegetable broth
- 1 can black beans, drained and rinsed
- 1 red bell pepper, diced
- 1 small red onion, diced
- 2 cloves garlic, minced
- 1 tablespoon olive oil
- 1 teaspoon cumin
- Salt and pepper, to taste
- Optional: avocado, salsa, and shredded cheese for topping

Directions:

1. Cook the quinoa: In a medium saucepan, bring the quinoa and water or broth to a boil. Reduce the heat to low, cover, and simmer for 15-20 minutes, or until the quinoa is tender and fluffy.
2. Heat the oil in a skillet: In a large skillet, heat the olive oil over medium-high heat.
3. Cook the vegetables: Add the diced bell pepper, onion, and garlic to the skillet. Cook, stirring occasionally, until the vegetables are tender, about 5-7 minutes.

4. Add the black beans and cumin: Stir in the black beans and cumin. Cook for 1-2 minutes, until heated through.
5. Assemble the bowls: Divide the cooked quinoa among four to six bowls. Top with the vegetable and black bean mixture.
6. Add toppings (optional): Add diced avocado, salsa, and shredded cheese, if desired.
7. Serve: Serve the gluten-free quinoa and black bean bowls hot, garnished with chopped fresh cilantro or scallions, if desired.

Tips:

- Use a variety of colorful vegetables to add visual appeal and nutrients to the dish.
- Substitute the quinoa with brown rice or cauliflower rice for a different texture.
- Experiment with different spices and seasonings, such as chili powder or smoked paprika, to add unique flavors to the dish.

Variations:

- Add some heat with diced jalapeños or serrano peppers.
- Use different types of beans, such as kidney beans or pinto beans, for a change of pace.
- Make the dish more substantial by adding cooked chicken, steak, or tofu.

Heart-Healthy Dishes

Serving Size: 4 servings

Prep Time: 15 minutes

Cooking Time: 12-15 minutes

Total Time: 27-30 minutes

Nutrition Information (per serving):

- Calories: 320
- Fat: 18g
- Saturated Fat: 3.5g
- Cholesterol: 60mg
- Sodium: 200mg
- Carbohydrates: 10g
- Fiber: 7g
- Sugar: 2g

- Protein: 35g

Ingredients:

- 4 salmon fillets (6 ounces each)
- 2 ripe avocados, diced
- 1 red onion, diced
- 1 jalapeño pepper, seeded and finely chopped
- 1 lime, juiced
- 2 cloves garlic, minced
- Salt and pepper, to taste
- Optional: chopped fresh cilantro for garnish

Directions:

1. Preheat the grill: Preheat the grill to medium-high heat.
2. Season the salmon: Season the salmon fillets with salt and pepper.
3. Grill the salmon: Grill the salmon for 4-5 minutes per side, or until cooked through.
4. Make the avocado salsa: In a medium bowl, combine the diced avocado, red onion, jalapeño pepper, lime juice, and garlic.
5. Serve: Serve the grilled salmon with the avocado salsa spooned over the top. Garnish with chopped fresh cilantro, if desired.

Tips:

- Use wild-caught salmon for the best flavor and nutrition.
- Substitute the salmon with other heart-healthy fish, such as tuna or mackerel.
- Experiment with different spices and seasonings, such as cumin or smoked paprika, to add unique flavors to the dish.

Variations:

- Add some heat with diced serrano peppers or red pepper flakes.
- Use different types of citrus, such as lemon or orange, for a different flavor profile.
- Make the dish more substantial by serving the grilled salmon with a side of quinoa or brown rice.

Heart-Healthy Benefits:

- Salmon is high in omega-3 fatty acids, which can help lower triglycerides and blood pressure.
- Avocados are rich in monounsaturated fats, which can help lower cholesterol and improve heart health.
- This dish is low in sodium and saturated fat, making it a heart-healthy option.

Vegan Air Fryer Meals

Serving Size: 4-6 servings

Prep Time: 10 minutes

Cooking Time: 12-15 minutes

Total Time: 22-25 minutes

Nutrition Information (per serving):

- Calories: 120
- Fat: 7g
- Saturated Fat: 1g
- Cholesterol: 0mg
- Sodium: 200mg
- Carbohydrates: 15g
- Fiber: 5g
- Sugar: 5g
- Protein: 3g

Ingredients:

- 1 head of cauliflower, broken into florets
- 1/2 cup vegan buffalo sauce (such as Annie's Naturals)
- 1 tablespoon olive oil
- 1 teaspoon garlic powder
- 1 teaspoon onion powder
- Salt and pepper, to taste
- Optional: chopped fresh cilantro or scallions for garnish

Directions:

1. Preheat the air fryer: Preheat the air fryer to 400°F (200°C).
2. Prepare the cauliflower: In a large bowl, toss the cauliflower florets with the olive oil, garlic powder, onion powder, salt, and pepper until they are evenly coated.
3. Cook the cauliflower: Place the cauliflower florets in the air fryer basket and cook for 12-15 minutes, or until tender and lightly browned, shaking the basket halfway through.
4. Toss with buffalo sauce: In a large bowl, toss the cooked cauliflower with the vegan buffalo sauce until they are evenly coated.
5. Serve: Serve the vegan air fryer cauliflower "wings" hot, garnished with chopped fresh cilantro or scallions if desired.

Tips:

- Use a variety of vegan sauces, such as BBQ or teriyaki, to change up the flavor.
- Experiment with different seasonings, such as smoked paprika or dried thyme, to add depth to the dish.
- Make the dish more substantial by serving the cauliflower "wings" with a side of vegan ranch dressing or a salad.

Variations:

- Add some crunch with chopped nuts or seeds.
- Use different types of vegetables, such as broccoli or carrots, for a change of pace.
- Make the dish more substantial by adding cooked chickpeas or tofu.

Low-Sodium Recipes

Serving Size: 4-6 servings

Prep Time: 15 minutes

Cooking Time: 15-20 minutes

Total Time: 30-35 minutes

Nutrition Information (per serving):

- Calories: 180
- Fat: 4g
- Saturated Fat: 1g
- Cholesterol: 60mg
- Sodium: 150mg
- Carbohydrates: 20g
- Fiber: 5g
- Sugar: 5g
- Protein: 25g

Ingredients:

- 1 pound boneless, skinless chicken breast, cut into bite-sized pieces
- 2 cups mixed vegetables (such as broccoli, bell peppers, carrots, and snap peas)

- 2 tablespoons olive oil
- 1 tablespoon low-sodium soy sauce (such as Bragg's)
- 1 teaspoon grated ginger
- 1 teaspoon garlic powder
- Salt-free seasoning blend (such as Mrs. Dash), to taste
- Optional: chopped fresh herbs (such as cilantro or scallions) for garnish

Directions:

1. Heat the oil in a skillet: Heat the olive oil in a large skillet or wok over medium-high heat.
2. Cook the chicken: Add the chicken to the skillet and cook until browned and cooked through, about 5-7 minutes. Remove from the skillet and set aside.
3. Cook the vegetables: Add the mixed vegetables to the skillet and cook until tender-crisp, about 3-5 minutes.
4. Make the sauce: In a small bowl, whisk together the low-sodium soy sauce, grated ginger, garlic powder, and salt-free seasoning blend.
5. Combine the chicken and vegetables with the sauce: Add the cooked chicken back into the skillet with the vegetables and pour the sauce over the top. Stir to combine.
6. Serve: Serve the low-sodium chicken and vegetable stir-fry hot, garnished with chopped fresh herbs if desired.

Tips:

- Use fresh herbs and spices to add flavor without adding salt.
- Experiment with different low-sodium sauces and seasonings to find the ones you like best.
- Make the dish more substantial by serving the stir-fry with brown rice or whole grain noodles.

Variations:

- Add some heat with diced jalapeños or serrano peppers.
- Use different types of protein, such as tofu or shrimp, for a change of pace.
- Make the dish more substantial by adding cooked quinoa or farro.

High-Protein Air Fryer Dishes

Serving Size: 4 servings

Prep Time: 10 minutes

Cooking Time: 12-15 minutes

Total Time: 22-25 minutes

Nutrition Information (per serving):

- Calories: 320
- Fat: 12g
- Saturated Fat: 3.5g
- Cholesterol: 80mg
- Sodium: 350mg
- Carbohydrates: 5g
- Fiber: 0g
- Sugar: 0g
- Protein: 40g

Ingredients:

- 4 boneless, skinless chicken breasts
- 6 slices of turkey bacon, cut into small pieces
- 1 tablespoon olive oil
- 1 teaspoon garlic powder
- 1 teaspoon onion powder
- Salt and pepper, to taste
- Optional: chopped fresh herbs (such as parsley or thyme) for garnish

Directions:

1. Preheat the air fryer: Preheat the air fryer to 375°F (190°C).
2. Prepare the chicken: In a small bowl, mix together the olive oil, garlic powder, onion powder, salt, and pepper. Brush the mixture evenly onto both sides of the chicken breasts.
3. Cook the chicken: Place the chicken breasts in the air fryer basket and cook for 10-12 minutes, or until cooked through.
4. Cook the turkey bacon: Place the turkey bacon pieces in the air fryer basket and cook for 2-3 minutes, or until crispy.
5. Assemble the dish: Top each cooked chicken breast with a few pieces of crispy turkey bacon.
6. Serve: Serve the high-protein air fryer chicken breast with turkey bacon hot, garnished with chopped fresh herbs if desired.

Tips:

- Use different types of protein, such as steak or tofu, for a change of pace.
- Experiment with different seasonings and spices, such as paprika or cumin, to add unique flavors to the dish.
- Make the dish more substantial by serving the chicken breast with a side of roasted vegetables or quinoa.

Variations:

- Add some heat with diced jalapeños or serrano peppers.
- Use different types of bacon, such as pork bacon or vegan bacon, for a different flavor.
- Make the dish more substantial by adding cooked eggs or black beans.

Chapter 7

Desserts

Air Fryer Donuts

Servings: 6-8 donuts
Cooking Time: 4-5 minutes per batch
Prep Time: 20 minutes
Nutrition Information (per serving):

- Calories: 120
- Fat: 2g
- Saturated Fat: 0.5g
- Cholesterol: 10mg
- Sodium: 100mg
- Carbohydrates: 25g
- Fiber: 1g
- Sugar: 10g
- Protein: 2g

Ingredients:

- 1 cup all-purpose flour
- 1/2 cup granulated sugar
- 1/2 cup whole milk
- 2 teaspoons active dry yeast
- 1/4 teaspoon salt
- 2 large eggs
- 2 tablespoons unsalted butter, melted
- Flavorings such as cinnamon, nutmeg, or vanilla extract (optional)
- Confectioners' sugar for dusting (optional)

Directions:

1. Proof the yeast: In a small bowl, combine the warm milk (about 105°F to 115°F) and yeast. Stir to dissolve the yeast, then let it sit for 5-10 minutes, or until frothy.
2. Combine dry ingredients: In a large bowl, whisk together the flour, sugar, and salt.
3. Add wet ingredients: Add the eggs, melted butter, and yeast mixture to the dry ingredients. Mix until a smooth batter forms.
4. Knead the dough: Using a stand mixer with a dough hook attachment or a wooden spoon, knead the dough for 5-7 minutes, until it becomes smooth and elastic.

5. Let the dough rise: Place the dough in a greased bowl, cover it with plastic wrap or a damp towel, and let it rise in a warm place for about 1 hour, or until it has doubled in size.

6. Punch down the dough: Once the dough has risen, punch it down to release any air bubbles.

7. Cut out the donuts: Use a donut cutter or a glass to cut out the donuts. You should be able to get about 6-8 donuts.

8. Air fry the donuts: Preheat the air fryer to 375°F (190°C). Place 2-3 donuts in the air fryer basket, leaving some space between them. Cook the donuts for 4-5 minutes, or until they are golden brown and cooked through. Repeat with the remaining donuts.

9. Dust with confectioners' sugar (optional): Once the donuts are cooked, dust them with confectioners' sugar for an extra touch of sweetness.

10. Serve and enjoy: Serve the Air Fryer Donuts warm and enjoy!

Chocolate Chip Cookies

Servings: 12-15 cookies
Cooking Time: 10-12 minutes
Prep Time: 10 minutes

Nutrition Information (per serving):

- Calories: 120
- Fat: 7g
- Saturated Fat: 4g
- Cholesterol: 10mg
- Sodium: 50mg
- Carbohydrates: 15g
- Fiber: 0g
- Sugar: 8g
- Protein: 1g

Ingredients:

- 2 1/4 cups all-purpose flour
- 1 tsp baking soda
- 1 tsp salt
- 1 cup unsalted butter, at room temperature
- 3/4 cup white granulated sugar
- 3/4 cup brown sugar
- 2 large eggs
- 2 cups semi-sweet chocolate chips

- Optional: nuts (walnuts or pecans work well)

Directions:

1. Preheat your oven: Set your oven to 375°F (190°C). Line a baking sheet with parchment paper or a silicone mat.
2. Whisk dry ingredients: In a medium bowl, whisk together the flour, baking soda, and salt. Set aside.
3. Cream butter and sugars: In a large bowl, use an electric mixer to cream together the butter and sugars until light and fluffy, about 2-3 minutes.
4. Add eggs: Beat in the eggs one at a time, making sure each egg is fully incorporated before adding the next.
5. Mix in dry ingredients: Gradually mix in the dry ingredients (flour mixture) until just combined, being careful not to overmix.
6. Stir in chocolate chips: Stir in the chocolate chips and nuts (if using).
7. Scoop and bake: Scoop tablespoon-sized balls of dough onto the prepared baking sheet, leaving about 2 inches of space between each cookie.
8. Bake: Bake for 10-12 minutes, or until the edges are lightly golden brown and the centers are set.
9. Cool: Remove the cookies from the oven and let them cool on the baking sheet for 5 minutes before transferring them to a wire rack to cool completely.

Tips and Variations:

- For chewier cookies, bake for 8-10 minutes. For crisper cookies, bake for 12-14 minutes.
- Add-ins like nuts, dried cranberries, or candy pieces can enhance the flavor and texture of your cookies.
- For a more intense chocolate flavor, use dark or bittersweet chocolate chips.

Apple Turnovers

Serving Size: 8-10 turnovers
Cooking Time: 25-30 minutes
Prep Time: 20-25 minutes

Nutrition Information (per serving):

- Calories: 220
- Fat: 10g
- Saturated Fat: 6g
- Cholesterol: 10mg
- Sodium: 150mg
- Carbohydrates: 30g

- Fiber: 2g
- Sugar: 15g
- Protein: 2g

Ingredients:

For the Pastry Dough:

- 2 cups all-purpose flour
- 1 teaspoon salt
- 1/2 cup cold unsalted butter, cut into small pieces
- 1/4 cup ice-cold water

For the Filling:

- 2-3 apples, peeled and sliced
- 1/2 cup granulated sugar
- 2 tablespoons all-purpose flour
- 1 teaspoon cinnamon
- 1/4 teaspoon nutmeg
- 1/4 teaspoon salt
- 1 tablespoon unsalted butter, melted

Directions:

1. Make the Pastry Dough: In a large bowl, combine the flour and salt. Add the cold butter and use a pastry blender or your fingers to work the butter into the flour until it resembles coarse crumbs. Gradually add the ice-cold water, stirring with a fork until the dough comes together in a ball. Wrap the dough in plastic wrap and refrigerate for at least 30 minutes.
2. Prepare the Filling: In a separate bowl, combine the sliced apples, granulated sugar, flour, cinnamon, nutmeg, and salt. Mix until the apples are evenly coated with the dry ingredients.
3. Assemble the Turnovers: On a lightly floured surface, roll out the chilled pastry dough to a thickness of about 1/8 inch. Cut out squares of dough, about 4 inches per side.
4. Place the Filling: Spoon a small amount of the apple filling onto one half of each square, leaving a 1/2-inch border around the edges.
5. Fold and Seal: Fold the other half of the dough square over the filling, pressing the edges to seal. Use a fork to crimp the edges and create a decorative border.
6. Brush with Egg Wash: Brush the tops of the turnovers with a beaten egg mixed with a little water.
7. Bake: Preheat your oven to 375°F (190°C). Place the turnovers on a baking sheet lined with parchment paper, leaving about 1 inch of space between each turnover. Bake for 25-30 minutes, or until the pastry is golden brown.
8. Serve: Serve the Apple Turnovers warm, dust with powdered sugar, or enjoy with a scoop of vanilla ice cream.

Berry Crumble

Serving Size: 6-8 servings
Cooking Time: 35-40 minutes
Prep Time: 15-20 minutes

Nutrition Information (per serving):

- Calories: 250
- Fat: 10g
- Saturated Fat: 2g
- Cholesterol: 10mg
- Sodium: 50mg
- Carbohydrates: 40g
- Fiber: 4g
- Sugar: 20g
- Protein: 2g

Ingredients:

For the Filling:

- 2 cups mixed berries (strawberries, blueberries, raspberries, blackberries)
- 1/4 cup granulated sugar
- 2 tablespoons cornstarch
- 1 tablespoon lemon juice
- 1/4 teaspoon salt

For the Topping:

- 1 cup rolled oats
- 1/2 cup brown sugar
- 1/2 cup chopped almonds (optional)
- 1/2 teaspoon cinnamon
- 1/4 teaspoon nutmeg
- 1/4 teaspoon salt
- 1/2 cup cold unsalted butter, cut into small pieces

Directions:

1. Preheat your oven: Set your oven to 375°F (190°C).
2. Prepare the filling: In a large bowl, combine the mixed berries, granulated sugar, cornstarch, lemon juice, and salt. Mix until the berries are evenly coated with the dry ingredients.

3. Transfer the filling: Transfer the berry mixture to a 9x9-inch baking dish.
4. Prepare the topping: In a separate bowl, combine the rolled oats, brown sugar, chopped almonds (if using), cinnamon, nutmeg, and salt. Mix until well combined.
5. Add the butter: Add the cold butter to the topping mixture and use your fingers or a pastry blender to work the butter into the dry ingredients until the mixture resembles coarse crumbs.
6. Top the filling: Spread the topping mixture evenly over the berry filling.
7. Bake: Bake the Berry Crumble for 35-40 minutes, or until the topping is golden brown and the filling is bubbly and tender.
8. Serve: Serve the Berry Crumble warm, topped with vanilla ice cream or whipped cream if desired.

Tips and Variations:

- Use fresh or frozen berries for this recipe. If using frozen, thaw and pat dry with paper towels before using.
- Add a splash of vanilla extract or a pinch of salt to the filling for extra flavor.
- Substitute other types of sugar, such as honey or maple syrup, for a different flavor profile.
- Make individual servings in ramekins or mini cast-iron skillets for a fun and easy dessert.

Churros with Dipping Sauce

Serving Size: 8-10 churros with dipping sauce
Cooking Time: 20-25 minutes
Prep Time: 20-25 minutes

Nutrition Information (per serving):

- Calories: 250
- Fat: 12g
- Saturated Fat: 8g
- Cholesterol: 10mg
- Sodium: 100mg
- Carbohydrates: 35g
- Fiber: 2g
- Sugar: 20g
- Protein: 2g

Ingredients:

For the Churros:

- 2 1/4 cups all-purpose flour

- 1/2 cup granulated sugar
- 1/2 teaspoon salt
- 1/4 teaspoon ground cinnamon
- 1/2 cup whole milk
- 2 large eggs
- Vegetable oil for frying
- Cinnamon sugar for coating (see below)

For the Dipping Sauce:

- 1 cup heavy cream
- 1/2 cup granulated sugar
- 2 tablespoons unsweetened cocoa powder
- 2 tablespoons unsalted butter
- 2 ounces high-quality dark chocolate (at least 70% cocoa), finely chopped

For the Cinnamon Sugar:

- 1/2 cup granulated sugar
- 2 tablespoons ground cinnamon

Directions:

1. Make the churro dough: In a medium saucepan, combine the milk, sugar, and salt. Heat over medium heat, stirring occasionally, until the sugar has dissolved and the mixture is hot but not boiling.
2. Remove from heat: Remove the saucepan from the heat and let it cool slightly.
3. Add flour and eggs: Add the flour to the saucepan and stir until combined. Let the mixture cool for 5-10 minutes, then add the eggs one at a time, stirring until each egg is fully incorporated before adding the next.
4. Knead the dough: Turn the dough out onto a floured surface and knead for 5-10 minutes, until the dough is smooth and elastic.
5. Rest the dough: Cover the dough with plastic wrap and let it rest for 30 minutes.
6. Fry the churros: Heat the vegetable oil in a deep frying pan or a deep fryer to 375°F (190°C). Pipe the dough through a star tip into 4-5 inch strips. Fry the churros for 2-3 minutes on each side, or until they are golden brown and puffed up.
7. Drain and coat: Remove the churros from the oil with a slotted spoon and place them on a paper towel-lined plate to drain excess oil. Coat the churros in cinnamon sugar while still warm.
8. Make the dipping sauce: In a small saucepan, combine the heavy cream, granulated sugar, and cocoa powder. Heat over medium heat, stirring occasionally, until the sugar has dissolved and the mixture is hot but not boiling.
9. Add chocolate and butter: Remove the saucepan from the heat and add the chopped chocolate and butter. Stir until the chocolate has melted and the sauce is smooth.
10. Serve: Serve the churros warm with the dipping sauce on the side.

Tips and Variations:

- For an extra crispy coating, chill the churros in the refrigerator for 30 minutes before frying.
- Experiment with different flavors by adding a teaspoon of vanilla extract or a pinch of salt to the dough.
- For a lighter coating, use powdered sugar instead of cinnamon sugar.
- Make the dipping sauce ahead of time and refrigerate for up to 3 days. Reheat before serving.

Air Fryer Brownies

Serving Size: 4-6 brownies
Cooking Time: 8-10 minutes
Prep Time: 10 minutes

Nutrition Information (per serving):

- Calories: 220
- Fat: 12g
- Saturated Fat: 8g
- Cholesterol: 20mg
- Sodium: 50mg
- Carbohydrates: 25g
- Fiber: 2g
- Sugar: 18g
- Protein: 3g

Ingredients:

- 1 and 1/2 sticks of unsalted butter (12 tablespoons), plus more for greasing
- 2 cups of sugar
- 4 large eggs
- 1/2 cup of unsweetened cocoa powder
- 1 teaspoon of vanilla extract
- 1 and 1/4 cups of all-purpose flour
- 1 teaspoon of salt
- 1 cup of semi-sweet chocolate chips
- Optional: nuts, espresso powder, or other mix-ins of your choice

Directions:

1. Preheat the air fryer: Set the air fryer to 375°F (190°C).

2. Grease the basket: Lightly grease the air fryer basket with butter or cooking spray.
3. Mix the batter: In a medium bowl, whisk together the flour, salt, and cocoa powder. Set aside.
4. Combine wet ingredients: In a large bowl, use an electric mixer to cream together the butter and sugar. Beat in the eggs one at a time, followed by the vanilla extract.
5. Combine wet and dry ingredients: Gradually mix the dry ingredients into the wet ingredients until just combined.
6. Stir in chocolate chips and mix-ins (if using): Fold in the chocolate chips and any desired mix-ins.
7. Pour the batter into the air fryer basket: Pour the batter into the prepared air fryer basket and smooth the top.
8. Cook the brownies: Cook the brownies in the air fryer for 8-10 minutes, or until a toothpick inserted into the center comes out with a few moist crumbs attached.
9. Let cool and cut: Remove the brownies from the air fryer and let cool completely in the basket. Cut into squares and serve.

Tips and Variations:

- For a chewier texture, cook the brownies for 6-8 minutes. For a firmer texture, cook for 10-12 minutes.
- Add-ins like nuts, espresso powder, or dried fruit can enhance the flavor and texture of the brownies.
- If you don't have an air fryer, you can also make these brownies in a traditional oven at 350°F (180°C) for 20-25 minutes.

Baked Pears with Cinnamon

Serving Size: 4-6 servings
Cooking Time: 25-30 minutes
Prep Time: 10-15 minutes

Nutrition Information (per serving):

- Calories: 120
- Fat: 0g
- Saturated Fat: 0g
- Cholesterol: 0mg
- Sodium: 10mg
- Carbohydrates: 30g
- Fiber: 4g
- Sugar: 20g
- Protein: 0g

Ingredients:

- 4-6 ripe pears (Bartlett or Anjou work well)
- 2 tablespoons unsalted butter
- 1/2 teaspoon ground cinnamon
- 1/4 teaspoon ground nutmeg
- 1/4 teaspoon salt
- 1 tablespoon honey or maple syrup (optional)

Directions:

1. Preheat your oven: Set your oven to 375°F (190°C).
2. Peel and core the pears: Peel, core, and halve the pears.
3. Mix the cinnamon mixture: In a small bowl, mix together the cinnamon, nutmeg, and salt.
4. Butter the pears: Dot the top of each pear half with unsalted butter.
5. Sprinkle with cinnamon mixture: Sprinkle the cinnamon mixture evenly over the pears.
6. Bake the pears: Place the pears on a baking sheet lined with parchment paper and bake for 25-30 minutes, or until the pears are tender and caramelized.
7. Drizzle with honey or maple syrup (optional): If desired, drizzle the baked pears with honey or maple syrup.
8. Serve: Serve the Baked Pears with Cinnamon warm, topped with whipped cream or vanilla ice cream if desired.

Tips and Variations:

- Use a variety of pear types, such as Bartlett, Anjou, or Bosc, for a unique flavor and texture.
- Add a splash of vanilla extract or a pinch of ground ginger to the cinnamon mixture for extra flavor.
- Serve the Baked Pears with Cinnamon as a topping for oatmeal or yogurt for a healthy breakfast option.
- Make ahead and reheat the pears in the microwave or oven when ready to serve.

Chapter 8

International Flavors

Italian Delights

Serving Size: 20-25 Italian Delights
Cooking Time: 2-3 minutes per batch
Prep Time: 20-25 minutes

Nutrition Information (per serving):

- Calories: 120
- Fat: 3g
- Saturated Fat: 0.5g
- Cholesterol: 0mg
- Sodium: 50mg
- Carbohydrates: 25g
- Fiber: 0g
- Sugar: 10g
- Protein: 2g

Ingredients:

- 2 cups all-purpose flour
- 2 teaspoons baking powder
- 1 teaspoon salt
- 1/4 cup granulated sugar
- 1/2 cup whole milk
- 2 large eggs
- Vegetable oil for frying
- Powdered sugar for dusting

Directions:

1. Combine dry ingredients: In a medium bowl, whisk together the flour, baking powder, and salt.
2. Combine wet ingredients: In a large bowl, whisk together the sugar, milk, and eggs.
3. Combine wet and dry ingredients: Gradually add the dry ingredients to the wet ingredients and mix until a smooth batter forms.
4. Heat the oil: Heat the vegetable oil in a deep frying pan or a deep fryer to 375°F (190°C).

5. Fry the dough balls: Using a cookie scoop or a spoon, drop the batter into the hot oil, making sure not to overcrowd the pan. Fry the dough balls for 2-3 minutes on each side, or until they are golden brown and puffed up.

6. Drain excess oil: Remove the fried dough balls from the oil with a slotted spoon and place them on a paper towel-lined plate to drain excess oil.

7. Dust with powdered sugar: Dust the Italian Delights with powdered sugar and serve warm.

Tips and Variations:

- For an extra crispy exterior, chill the batter in the refrigerator for 30 minutes before frying.
- Experiment with different flavors by adding a teaspoon of vanilla extract or a pinch of salt to the batter.
- Fill the Italian Delights with a sweet ricotta or cannoli cream filling for an extra-decadent treat.
- Serve the Italian Delights with a side of chocolate sauce or whipped cream for dipping.

Asian Inspirations

Serving Size: 4-6 servings
Cooking Time: 10-12 minutes
Prep Time: 15-20 minutes
Nutrition Information (per serving):

- Calories: 420
- Fat: 20g
- Saturated Fat: 8g
- Cholesterol: 20mg
- Sodium: 400mg
- Carbohydrates: 45g
- Fiber: 4g
- Sugar: 10g
- Protein: 15g

Ingredients:

- 1 cup rice noodles or soba noodles
- 2 tablespoons vegetable oil
- 1 onion, thinly sliced
- 2 cloves garlic, minced
- 1 cup mixed vegetables (bell peppers, carrots, broccoli)
- 1 cup cooked chicken, beef, or tofu
- 2 tablespoons soy sauce
- 1 tablespoon oyster sauce (optional)

- 1 tablespoon honey
- 1 teaspoon grated ginger
- Salt and pepper to taste
- Sesame seeds and chopped green onions for garnish (optional)

Directions:

1. Cook the noodles: Cook the rice noodles or soba noodles according to package instructions. Drain and set aside.
2. Heat the wok or large skillet: Heat 1 tablespoon of vegetable oil in a large skillet or wok over medium-high heat.
3. Stir-fry the onion and garlic: Add the sliced onion and minced garlic to the skillet and stir-fry until the onion is translucent.
4. Add the mixed vegetables: Add the mixed vegetables to the skillet and stir-fry for 2-3 minutes.
5. Add the cooked protein: Add the cooked chicken, beef, or tofu to the skillet and stir-fry for another minute.
6. Add the sauce ingredients: Add the soy sauce, oyster sauce (if using), honey, and grated ginger to the skillet. Stir-fry for another minute, until the sauce has thickened.
7. Combine the noodles and sauce: Add the cooked noodles to the skillet and stir-fry until the noodles are well coated with the sauce.
8. Season with salt and pepper: Season the noodles with salt and pepper to taste.
9. Garnish with sesame seeds and green onions (optional): Garnish the noodles with sesame seeds and chopped green onions (if using).
10. Serve: Serve the Asian-Style Stir-Fried Noodles hot, enjoy!

Tips and Variations:

- Customize the recipe to your taste by adding your favorite vegetables, protein, or sauce ingredients.
- Use different types of noodles, such as udon or ramen noodles, for a change of pace.
- Add a sprinkle of toasted sesame seeds or chopped nuts for added crunch and flavor.
- Serve the noodles with a side of steamed vegetables or a green salad for a well-rounded meal.

Mexican Favorites

Serving Size: 8-10 churros with cajeta sauce
Cooking Time: 2-3 minutes per batch
Prep Time: 20-25 minutes

Nutrition Information (per serving):

- Calories: 250

- Fat: 12g
- Saturated Fat: 8g
- Cholesterol: 10mg
- Sodium: 100mg
- Carbohydrates: 35g
- Fiber: 2g
- Sugar: 20g
- Protein: 2g

Ingredients:

For the Churros:

- 2 cups all-purpose flour
- 1/2 cup granulated sugar
- 1/2 teaspoon salt
- 1/4 teaspoon ground cinnamon
- 1/2 cup whole milk
- 2 large eggs
- Vegetable oil for frying
- Cinnamon sugar for coating (see below)

For the Cajeta Sauce:

- 1 cup goat's milk
- 1/2 cup granulated sugar
- 1/4 teaspoon sea salt
- 1/2 teaspoon vanilla extract

For the Cinnamon Sugar:

- 1/2 cup granulated sugar
- 2 tablespoons ground cinnamon

Directions:

1. Combine dry ingredients: In a medium bowl, whisk together the flour, sugar, salt, and cinnamon.
2. Combine wet ingredients: In a large bowl, whisk together the milk, eggs, and vanilla extract.
3. Combine wet and dry ingredients: Gradually add the dry ingredients to the wet ingredients and mix until a smooth batter forms.
4. Heat the oil: Heat the vegetable oil in a deep frying pan or a deep fryer to 375°F (190°C).
5. Fry the churros: Using a piping bag or a plastic bag with a corner cut off, pipe the batter into 4-5 inch strips. Fry the churros for 2-3 minutes on each side, or until they are golden brown and puffed up.

6. Drain excess oil: Remove the fried churros from the oil with a slotted spoon and place them on a paper towel-lined plate to drain excess oil.

7. Coat with cinnamon sugar: Coat the churros in cinnamon sugar while still warm.

8. Make the cajeta sauce: In a medium saucepan, combine the goat's milk, sugar, and sea salt. Heat over medium heat, stirring occasionally, until the sugar has dissolved and the mixture is hot but not boiling. Remove from heat and stir in the vanilla extract.

9. Serve: Serve the churros warm with the cajeta sauce for dipping.

Tips and Variations:

- For an extra crispy exterior, chill the batter in the refrigerator for 30 minutes before frying.
- Experiment with different flavors by adding a teaspoon of vanilla extract or a pinch of salt to the batter.
- Fill the churros with a sweet ricotta or cannoli cream filling for an extra-decadent treat.
- Serve the churros with a side of chocolate sauce or whipped cream for dipping.

Mediterranean Treats

Serving Size: 12-15 triangles
Cooking Time: 20-25 minutes
Prep Time: 20-25 minutes

Nutrition Information (per serving):

- Calories: 150
- Fat: 8g
- Saturated Fat: 2g
- Cholesterol: 10mg
- Sodium: 200mg
- Carbohydrates: 15g
- Fiber: 2g
- Sugar: 2g
- Protein: 5g

Ingredients:

- 1 package of filo dough (usually found in the freezer section)
- 1 cup fresh spinach, chopped
- 1 cup crumbled feta cheese
- 1/2 cup grated Parmesan cheese
- 1/4 cup chopped fresh parsley
- 2 cloves garlic, minced

- 1/2 teaspoon salt
- 1/4 teaspoon black pepper
- 2 tablespoons olive oil

Directions:

1. Thaw the filo dough: Thaw the filo dough according to the package instructions.
2. Prepare the filling: In a medium bowl, combine the chopped spinach, crumbled feta cheese, grated Parmesan cheese, chopped parsley, garlic, salt, and pepper. Mix well.
3. Assemble the triangles: Lay a sheet of filo dough on a flat surface and brush with olive oil. Place a tablespoon of the spinach and feta mixture in the center of the dough. Fold the dough over the filling to form a triangle and press the edges to seal. Repeat with the remaining dough and filling.
4. Brush with olive oil: Brush the tops of the triangles with olive oil.
5. Bake: Preheat the oven to 375°F (190°C). Place the triangles on a baking sheet lined with parchment paper and bake for 20-25 minutes, or until golden brown.
6. Serve: Serve the Mediterranean Treats warm or at room temperature.

Tips and Variations:

- Use fresh spinach for the best flavor and texture.
- Add some chopped sun-dried tomatoes or Kalamata olives to the filling for extra flavor.
- Use a combination of feta and ricotta cheese for a creamier filling.
- Serve the Mediterranean Treats with a side of tzatziki sauce or hummus for a delicious and refreshing snack.

Indian Spices

Serving Size: 4-6 servings
Cooking Time: 30-40 minutes
Prep Time: 15-20 minutes

Nutrition Information (per serving):

- Calories: 250
- Fat: 10g
- Saturated Fat: 1.5g
- Cholesterol: 0mg
- Sodium: 400mg
- Carbohydrates: 35g
- Fiber: 5g
- Sugar: 5g

- Protein: 10g

Ingredients:

- 1 can chickpeas (14 oz), drained and rinsed
- 2 medium onions, chopped
- 2 cloves garlic, minced
- 1 medium tomato, diced
- 1 teaspoon ground cumin
- 1 teaspoon ground coriander
- 1/2 teaspoon ground cinnamon
- 1/2 teaspoon ground cardamom
- 1/4 teaspoon ground cayenne pepper
- 1/2 teaspoon salt
- 1/4 teaspoon black pepper
- 2 tablespoons vegetable oil
- 2 tablespoons tomato puree
- 1 cup water
- Fresh cilantro, chopped (optional)

Directions:

1. Heat oil in a pan: Heat 1 tablespoon of oil in a large pan over medium heat.
2. Add onions and garlic: Add the chopped onions and minced garlic to the pan and cook until the onions are translucent.
3. Add spices: Add the cumin, coriander, cinnamon, cardamom, cayenne pepper, salt, and black pepper to the pan and cook for 1 minute.
4. Add tomato puree and water: Add the tomato puree and water to the pan and bring to a boil.
5. Add chickpeas: Add the chickpeas to the pan and simmer for 20-25 minutes, or until the sauce has thickened and the chickpeas are coated.
6. Taste and adjust: Taste and adjust the seasoning as needed.
7. Garnish with cilantro (optional): Garnish with chopped cilantro, if desired.
8. Serve: Serve the Chana Masala over basmati rice or with naan bread.

Tips and Variations:

- Use fresh tomatoes instead of tomato puree for a brighter flavor.
- Add some heat to the dish by increasing the amount of cayenne pepper.
- Use kidney beans or black beans instead of chickpeas for a different texture.
- Serve the Chana Masala with some raita (a yogurt and cucumber sauce) to cool down the palate.

French Classics

Serving Size: 4-6 ramekins
Cooking Time: 25-30 minutes
Prep Time: 20-25 minutes

Nutrition Information (per serving):

- Calories: 220
- Fat: 14g
- Saturated Fat: 8g
- Cholesterol: 100mg
- Sodium: 50mg
- Carbohydrates: 20g
- Fiber: 0g
- Sugar: 18g
- Protein: 3g

Ingredients:

- 2 cups heavy cream
- 1 cup granulated sugar
- 1/2 cup whole milk
- 1/4 cup granulated sugar (for caramelizing)
- 3 large egg yolks
- 1/2 teaspoon vanilla extract

Directions:

1. Preheat the oven: Preheat the oven to 300°F (150°C).
2. Combine the cream, sugar, and milk: In a medium saucepan, combine the heavy cream, granulated sugar, and whole milk. Heat over medium heat, stirring occasionally, until the sugar has dissolved and the mixture is hot but not boiling.
3. Temper the egg yolks: In a small bowl, whisk together the egg yolks and vanilla extract. Gradually add the warm cream mixture to the egg yolks, whisking constantly.
4. Pour into ramekins: Pour the mixture into 4-6 ramekins or small baking dishes.
5. Bake: Place the ramekins in a large baking dish and add hot water to come halfway up the sides of the ramekins. Bake for 25-30 minutes, or until the edges are set and the centers are still slightly jiggly.
6. Chill: Remove the ramekins from the water bath and let them cool to room temperature. Cover with plastic wrap and refrigerate for at least 2 hours or overnight.
7. Caramelize the sugar: Just before serving, sprinkle a thin layer of granulated sugar over the top of each ramekin. Caramelize the sugar with a kitchen torch or under the broiler.

Tips and Variations:

- Use high-quality ingredients, including farm-fresh eggs and real vanilla extract, for the best flavor and texture.
- Add a pinch of salt or a teaspoon of liqueur, such as Grand Marnier or Cognac, to the custard base for added depth of flavor.
- Experiment with different flavor combinations, such as adding a teaspoon of instant coffee or a pinch of cinnamon to the custard base.
- Serve the Crème Brûlée chilled, with a side of fresh fruit or a sprinkle of powdered sugar.

Middle Eastern Gems

Serving Size: 24-30 pieces
Cooking Time: 45-50 minutes
Prep Time: 20-25 minutes

Nutrition Information (per serving):

- Calories: 220
- Fat: 12g
- Saturated Fat: 2g
- Cholesterol: 0mg
- Sodium: 100mg
- Carbohydrates: 25g
- Fiber: 2g
- Sugar: 15g
- Protein: 3g

Ingredients:

- 1 package of phyllo dough (usually found in the freezer section)
- 1 cup chopped walnuts
- 1 cup chopped pistachios
- 1/2 cup granulated sugar
- 1/4 cup all-purpose flour
- 1/2 teaspoon ground cinnamon
- 1/4 teaspoon ground cardamom
- 1/4 teaspoon ground cloves
- 1/4 teaspoon salt
- 1/4 cup unsalted butter, melted

- 1 egg, beaten (for brushing phyllo dough)
- 1 tablespoon honey

Directions:

1. Thaw the phyllo dough: Thaw the phyllo dough according to the package instructions.
2. Prepare the nut mixture: In a medium bowl, combine the chopped walnuts, pistachios, granulated sugar, flour, cinnamon, cardamom, cloves, and salt. Mix well.
3. Assemble the baklava: Layer the phyllo dough, brushing each layer with melted butter, and sprinkle with the nut mixture.
4. Cut the baklava: Cut the baklava into diamond-shaped pieces.
5. Bake the baklava: Preheat the oven to 350°F (180°C). Bake the baklava for 45-50 minutes, or until golden brown.
6. Glaze with honey: Remove the baklava from the oven and let it cool for 10 minutes. Drizzle with honey and serve.

Tips and Variations:

- Use a combination of nuts, such as almonds and hazelnuts, for a different flavor.
- Add a sprinkle of rose water or orange blossom water to the nut mixture for a fragrant flavor.
- Use a honey syrup, made by boiling honey with water, to glaze the baklava.
- Serve the baklava with a cup of Turkish coffee or tea for a traditional Middle Eastern experience.

Printed in Great Britain
by Amazon

59797697R00051